Making It Work

Educating the Blind/Visually Impaired Student in the Regular School

**a volume in
Critical Concerns in Blindness**

Series Editor:
Ronald J. Ferguson, *Louisiana Tech University*

Critical Concerns in Blindness

Ronald J. Ferguson, Series Editor

The Blindness Revolution: Jernigan in His Own Words (2005)
   by James H. Omvig

Education and Rehabilitation for Empowerment (in prep 2005)
   by Ed Vaughan & James H. Omvig

Making It Work

Educating the Blind/Visually Impaired Student in the Regular School

by
Carol Castellano

INFORMATION AGE
PUBLISHING

Greenwich, Connecticut • www.infoagepub.com

Library of Congress Cataloging-in-Publication Data

Castellano, Carol, 1951-
  Making it work : educating the blind/visually impaired student in the
regular school / by Carol Castellano.
      p. cm. -- (Critical concerns in blindness)
  Includes bibliographical references and index.
  ISBN 1-59311-418-4 (pbk.) -- ISBN 1-59311-423-0 (hardcover)
  1. Children, Blind--Education--United States. 2. Children with
visual
disabilities--Education--United States. 3. Mainstreaming in
education--United States. I. Title. II. Series.
  HV1795.C37 2005
  371.91'1--dc22

Illustrations by Lynne Cucco
Cover design by Brittany Wolf and Arianne Petersen

Printed in the United States of America

To my mom Nancy and in memory of my dad John,
for always believing in us,
and to all the educators out there
who are making it work

"Why the regular school? Because there is not a 'sighted world' with blind people living outside it, but one world in which the blind person also lives. The blind person belongs; schools are for her or him, too, the same school, the same world, the same kind of life."

—Adrienne Asch
Henry R. Luce Professor in Biology, Ethics,
and the Politics of Human Reproduction
Wellesley College, Wellesley, MA
... and blind since birth.

"I've never seen a child who doesn't have a disability and I've never seen a child who doesn't have a gift. It's up to the team to get the best out of the child by teaching the child to compensate for the disability and to work with the gift."

—R. Bruce Padian
High School Principal

CONTENTS

ACKNOWLEDGMENTS

My heartfelt thanks go to the many people whose ideas and insights contributed to the writing of this book. I am grateful to Joanne Wilson, Ruby Ryles, and the Lions Clubs of Belleville, Bloomfield, and Nutley, NJ for getting the project started. My thanks go to Madeline Brooks, Barbara Cheadle, Meg Fornaro, RJ Fornaro, Barbara Shalit, Roseann Weinstein, and Sarah Weinstein, for reviewing the manuscript and offering comments, suggestions, and encouragement. Pam Cucco, Rick Fox, Luby Masi, John Masi, Pam Noblin, Donna Panaro, Valerie Ryan, and Linda Thomas provided invaluable information. Thanks to Larry Feinsod, Bruce Padian, Madeline Sinoway, Linda Kent, and John Connolly for spending time thinking and talking to me about the issues and for making it work for their students. I will be forever grateful to Jenelle Erickson for giving kids a chance in the regular school and I thank Sean, Connor, Michelle, and John, for inspiring their teachers.

Special thanks go to my dear friends Mina Albanese, Joe Cutter, Ellen Rice, and Gay Wilentz, my sister Barbara Castellana Stasiak, and my brother and sister-in-law Johnny and Marisa Castellano for helping me organize the material, offering time management tips, reading the manuscript, and always being willing to talk to me to discuss ideas or provide moral support, any time day or night. My loving thanks go to my mom Nancy Castellano for being my biggest fan, my daughter Serena for reading the manuscript, being enthusiastic, and providing the inspiration for it all, my son John for always having time to talk to me about words and ideas and for providing excellent editing advice, and to my husband Billy Cucco for putting up with late dinners and all the inconveniences of my crazy schedule and for valuing the work that I do.

CHAPTER 1

WHY THE REGULAR SCHOOL?

The education of blind students in the regular school in the United States has a long, proud history. It begins in 1900, when the first blind students entered public schools, and thus precedes P.L. 94-142 and the Individuals with Disabilities Education Act (IDEA) by 7 and a half decades!

The benefits to blind/visually impaired students who attend the regular school are manifold. First are the academic benefits—high standards, a wide choice of courses, including honors and advanced levels, and highly qualified teachers. Next are the social benefits—a wealth of clubs and activities, sports and music opportunities, and social events. In the regular school, blind/visually impaired students can learn how to handle themselves in the mainstream of life, the real world, in which they will eventually work and compete. Perhaps the most important benefit is growing up having the same experiences and having things in common with brothers and sisters, friends in the neighborhood, and friends in the wider world.

The blind/visually impaired student is not the only one to reap benefits. Classroom teachers report that the experience hones their own teaching skills and that the expanded verbal description and vocabulary enhances everyone's communication skills. In addition, increased opportunities for sensory learning provide a richer learning environment for all students in the class.

Making It Work: Educating the Blind/VI Student in the Regular School, 1–5
Copyright © 2005 by Information Age Publishing
All rights of reproduction in any form reserved.

THE EDUCATION OF BLIND CHILDREN: A BRIEF HISTORY

The very first time that blind children were able to receive a formal education occurred in Paris when a school for the blind was established in the 1780s. The founder of the school developed a way to emboss books and demonstrated for the first time that blind students could be educated and become literate. Louis Braille was among the students educated at this school and it was here that he developed his revolutionary reading and writing code. Following the success of the Paris institution, schools for the blind were established in other European countries. The first school for the blind in the United States was founded in 1829. By 1900, there were 40 such institutions.

These first schools were residential. Since the population of blind children was small and scattered and the production of books and materials slow and expensive, sending students to a centralized location seemed to be a practical solution. For most blind children, however, receiving an education meant having to leave home, often at the tender age of 6 or 7. As early as 1866, the head of the first American school for the blind recognized and publicly enumerated the flaws in the residential system, among them, the severing of family ties, the repression of individuality, and the perpetuation of the idea that greater differences between the sighted and the blind exist than really do (Samuel Gridley Howe in Koestler, 2004, p. 452).

In 1900, the first programs to enable blind children to attend public schools were established in several U.S. cities, where the population was large enough to support such an endeavor. The programs were a success, but remained few in number. The situation remained thus, with pockets of children being educated in public schools and most attending schools for the blind, until an advance in medical technology precipitated a huge change.

In the early 1940s a mysterious blindness began appearing among infants born prematurely. The search for reasons began immediately, but it was not until 1954 that the use of supplemental oxygen in incubators was found to be the cause. By that time, thousands of babies had become blind. This surge in the population of blind children would have overwhelmed the schools for the blind and for this and other reasons, blind children began entering public schools in record numbers. In the space of only 10 years, public schools became the established place for educating blind children and the residential schools began to evolve into schools specializing in blind children with additional disabilities. Today, approximately 85% of blind children, including those with additional disabilities, are enrolled in public schools.[1]

WHO ARE THE BLIND CHILDREN?

There are approximately 100,000 school-age blind and visually impaired children in the United States (less than .2% of the school-age population), making blindness/visual impairment in children a low-incidence disability.[2] Within this small population are even smaller subcategories. There are children who are totally blind and children who have some vision. Among those with vision, some have stable eyesight and others have conditions that will cause their eyesight to deteriorate. There are children for whom blindness/visual impairment is the only disability and others who have additional disabilities. Blindness in some children is part of a syndrome and can appear with other conditions which can range from mild to severe. In addition, blind/visually impaired children can fall anywhere in the intelligence range from genius to profoundly impaired.

Regardless of the many possible subcategories, for education purposes, it is useful to divide the population of blind/visually impaired children into three groups.

- First are blind/visually impaired children who have no other disabilities or whose other disabilities are mild and do not affect their education. These children will have the same academic goals as their sighted classmates and will be fully integrated into regular classrooms. The main adaptations needed will be materials adapted into tactile or enlarged form.
- The next group consists of blind/visually impaired children who have additional disabilities which require modifications to the curriculum in addition to materials in adapted form.
- In the third group are blind/visually impaired children with severe additional disabilities, who may require a completely individualized curriculum consisting primarily of developmental rather than academic goals.

BLIND OR VISUALLY IMPAIRED?

It often surprises educators and parents to learn that the vast majority of children who fit the legal and educational definitions of *blindness* actually have some—often a great deal of—usable vision. Each child falls somewhere along the range from 20/70 vision, which qualifies as visual impairment, to 20/200, which qualifies as legally blind, to totally blind. Only a very small percentage (about 10%) are totally or near totally blind. Whether blind or visually impaired, however, these children have educational needs in common—they need a way to read and write that enables them to keep up with the class; they need a way to take and read back their notes; they need a way to move independently and safely from one place to another; they need to develop the social skills necessary to make friends and interact in class; they need to develop independence in all areas.

Because of this set of shared needs and because students deserve access to the whole continuum of skills and tools that can address these needs, I have chosen to use the term *blind/visually impaired* or *blind/VI* when referring to the students, rather than categorizing some students as blind and others as visually impaired. I have also chosen not to classify the ideas and suggestions in this book as "for the blind student" or "for the visually impaired student." Not every idea in this book will be relevant for every child, but teachers should feel free to choose among all the skills and tools on the continuum—both visual and nonvisual—for the benefit of the student. It is not whether the student is *blind* or *visually impaired* that should determine whether visual or nonvisual techniques are taught. It is whether or not the student has an efficient, safe way to handle all of the tasks before him or her. (Please see A Skills Definition of Blindness, page 15, for further discussion of this subject.)

Likewise, it is not *how blind* a student is that should determine a child's educational placement. In fact, braille-using students—children who generally have less vision—are often better equipped to keep up in a regular classroom than their partially sighted peers for whom print is not an efficient reading medium. The law does not allow placement decisions to be made on the basis of a child's disability or its severity, but requires basing the decision on the setting that can best meet the student's educational needs and goals. And for most blind/visually impaired students since the mid-1950s, that setting has been the regular school.

One More Note on Terminology

The specialized teachers who teach braille and other skills of blindness/visual impairment to students are known by a variety of names, but for brevity's sake I have chosen to use the term *teacher of the visually impaired* which can be shortened to TVI. The term *O&M* is the standard abbreviated term for orientation and mobility. O&M instructors teach the use of the white cane and other travel techniques to blind/visually impaired students.

YOU CAN MAKE IT WORK

Blindness/visual impairment in children is rare, so chances are no one in your school district has had experience with such a student. The team will have to put some effort into setting up a good educational program; but seeing your student thrive will make the effort worthwhile. This book will guide you as you construct the program. Written in plain English, it will help demystify the education of a blind/visually impaired student and provide both guiding principles and nuts and bolts advice with which to put the program together. This book will not elucidate for you the intricacies, timetables, and mandates of the law—what you *have* to do. The aim is simply to offer practical advice and effective strategies—what you *can* do to make it work.

NOTES

1. According to the American Printing House for the Blind's (n.d.) "Distribution of Eligible Students Based on the Federal Quota Census of January 6, 2003 (Fiscal Year 2004)," of the 56,913 school children registered for APH services in 2003, 9% attended schools for the blind and 85% were served by their state department of education.
2. Approximate number of school-age blind children from Spungin and D'Andrea (2000, p. 453). Percentage calculated by author from 2003 U.S. census figures.

CHAPTER 2

RAISING EXPECTATIONS

Most sighted people believe that blind people need a lot of help. It's almost always the first reaction people have when they meet a young blind child—"How can I help this dear, sweet, *helpless* child?" Even some sensitivity exercises, designed to develop awareness and understanding of blindness, have as an explicit goal—the understanding of what it is like to be helpless.

What do *you* believe about blindness? How do you feel about blindness and the blind/visually impaired child you will be working with every day? Do blind people need a lot of help? Are blind people limited in certain ways? Can blind people know as much as sighted people? Does a blind person lead a lonely existence in the dark? Does it take courage to live as a blind person? Is blindness a tragedy? Do blind people need our compassion?

Our beliefs are important because what we believe influences what we do. Our beliefs about blindness will affect the way we act toward the blind children with whom we work—the way we teach them, the messages we give them, our expectations for what they can achieve.

Why do so many sighted people believe that blind people are helpless? I think it's because sighted people cannot imagine doing things without eyesight. We use it almost all the time. It is certainly our overriding sense. If we close our eyes and picture ourselves trying to do something without eyesight, we feel we would be unable to accomplish even the simplest task. Sighted people tend to think that anyone who can accomplish *anything* without sight is extraordinary or amazing.

Even professionals in the blindness field who work with and write about blind/VI people often base their conclusions *on what they believe blindness must be like*—the difficulties, deficiencies, and frustrations they believe blind/VI people must have. These negative assumptions, based on the idea that the life of a blind/VI person is necessarily inferior to that of a sighted person, truly constitute a *sighted bias*. Unfortunately, this bias permeates much of the professional literature on blindness.

What if I were to lose my eyesight tomorrow? I would be relatively helpless … at first. What would I need to do? I would need to learn *the skills and tools of blindness*. The skills and tools of blindness/visual impairment are the ways in which blind/VI people manage the tasks of daily life simply, safely, and efficiently. They enable blind/VI people to accomplish tasks without frustration and with success. The skills and tools of blindness/visual impairment are the key to being able to function competitively. The more teachers and other school personnel learn about the skills and tools the blind/VI student will be using, the more they will be able to help the student succeed in school and in life.

ASSUMPTIONS

Does it take courage to live as a blind/VI person? Many sighted people think it does. Perhaps they feel that they would be very frightened if they had to go through life without eyesight and therefore they assume it takes courage to live life in that way. Heading toward an open stairway, going down an escalator, or crossing a busy street without eyesight might seem frightening or even unimaginable to a sighted person, and therefore anyone who attempts such feats must be courageous. But for blind/VI children, being blind/VI is natural. From the start they are learning skills and using tools that enable them to live life normally–to go down steps, use escalators, and cross streets safely. There is nothing strange or frightening about life for blind/VI children, and therefore it does not take courage for them to live.

Is blindness a tragedy, a terrible loss? Most blind/VI children have *not* experienced a loss of sight. Again, being blind/VI is natural for them. They are not constantly making comparisons to sight. Blind/VI children are not thinking in terms of loss. (Think about this when you hear blindness/visual impairment referred to as vision loss.) They are not walking around all day wishing they were sighted or expending their energy lamenting a sense they do not have. They are too busy living and learning! While there is indeed a psychological adjustment that people must make if they *become* blind/VI, even children who do lose their sight seem to adjust quickly. One blind scientist reports that after going from partial vision to total blindness at age 3, "my world was not black and hopeless. It sparkled as it did before, but now with sounds, odors, shapes, and textures" (Vermeij, 1997, p. 14).

Blind/VI children are simply doing what all children do—living and learning and developing and growing. Life is a *positive* process to them, not a negative one. We adults can certainly *make* a blind/VI child feel lacking and inferior and inadequate. We can also choose to make the child feel whole, equal, and competent. It is our attitudes that will shape so much of the blind/VI child's experience. Therefore it is up to the adults in the child's life to learn and express positive attitudes about blindness/visual impairment and the abilities of blind/VI people.

Are blind people actually living in the dark? (And we know that many sighted people are notoriously afraid of the dark.) When asked if she saw only darkness, one blind woman put it this way: "Close your eyes. Think about what your nose sees." "My nose doesn't see at all," responded her companion. "Well," returned the blind woman, "that's how it is with my eyes."

Often sighted people are convinced that blind/VI people are in danger—after all, they cannot see where they are going. What if they fall down the steps? What if there is an obstacle in the way? Once again, blind/VI people use skills and tools to navigate safely and *knowledgeably* through the environment. For example, a cane can identify obstacles, find a clear path, locate a doorway, detect stairs up and down. Many blind/VI people learn to *hear* objects and spaces in the environment like doorway openings and intersecting hallways. In fact, it is possible to give directions to a blind/VI person such as "listen for the open doorway on the left. The library is the wooden door right after it. You'll know you're in the right place if you find a carpeted floor." (Through the cane the blind/VI person can perceive the difference in floor texture.) (More on travel skills can be found in The Skills and Tools of Blindness, page 38.)

Blind/VI adults use the skills and tools of blindness/visual impairment every day to travel independently to jobs, classes, meetings, and whatever other endeavors they are involved in. They might use a cane or a guide dog; surely they are listening carefully, paying attention, and using problem-solving techniques. They are well aware of potential dangers in the environment and have learned skills to deal with them. Once again, skills and tools are the key. Make sure your student gets the opportunity to learn, practice, and master these skills.

Is it frustrating to be blind/VI? Sometimes teachers and parents report that the blind/VI child becomes frustrated and angry when trying to accomplish a certain task or throws a tantrum when he or she is unable to go along with the other children. Often, however, when we examine cases like this, we find that no one has taught the child the *skill* that would enable him or her to accomplish the task or keep up with the others. The tendency is to blame blindness when in reality it is lack of skills that is causing the problem.

This phenomenon occurs also with adults who have lost some of their vision. Trying fruitlessly to complete tasks using only their now impaired vision, they assume that their difficulties and frustrations are due to the visual impairment, instead of due to the lack of training in alternative skills. Once they realize that a nonvisual skill can help them, they no longer have to rely on their less than adequate eyesight. The new skill sets them free by equipping them with competence, confidence, and independence.

Sometimes it is sighted adults who inadvertently impose a barrier on the blind/VI child. One mom of twins told me that her young blind daughter was becoming very frustrated at being blind. When I observed the situation in person, I saw that without realizing it, the mom was allowing her sighted twin to move freely throughout the house, including up and down the steps, but she was prohibiting her blind twin from doing the same thing. It was not blindness that was frustrating the girl, but being held back.

When I pointed this out to the mom, she said that her daughter might get hurt if she went up and down the steps. The mom mistakenly assumed that eyesight was necessary in order to go up and down steps safely and she acted on her assumption. Once this parent learned that blind/VI people can indeed handle steps safely, she was very willing to have her child learn how. When the child learned the skill of safely navigating steps, the mom gave her the run of the house and the frustration disappeared.

How will the blind/VI child learn? After all, isn't 80% of learning visual? Well, the good news is *this statistic only applies to sighted people!* Blind/VI children are able to learn everything their sighted peers of similar cognitive ability learn, but they will learn it using their hands, their ears, their senses of taste and smell, and whatever eyesight they may have. Blindness/visual impairment is *not* a learning disability. It does *not* affect the student's ability to understand. The brain is an equal opportunity employer; it does not care which avenue the information comes in through! (Cutter, 2004).

One learning consultant in private practice believed she was very open regarding the abilities of students with disabilities. Yet she automatically ruled out geometry and physics for a blind/VI student, *assuming* that these subjects were visual and that eyesight was necessary for understanding them. The consultant was not conscious of her sighted bias until the child's parents challenged her assumption. In reality, it is only the usual presentation of those subjects that is visual. The concepts can certainly be presented in alternative ways and perceived through other senses. The understanding takes place in the brain, both for the sighted and the blind/VI student.

DEVELOPING POSITIVE ATTITUDES

We have choices in the way we view blindness/visual impairment. We can view the blind/VI student as helpless—or we can choose a can-do approach and teach the student skills. We can believe that blindness/visual impairment is sad and we can feel sorry for the student, or we can decide it's okay to be blind/visually impaired. We can blame blindness for any lack of achievement or problem in school or we can search for the real culprit which might be a lack of appropriate materials or a lack of training in a skill. We can focus on blindness/visual impairment as a deficit in the child or we can choose the path of normalization, viewing the blind/VI student as a *regular* kid. But before we can choose these positive approaches, we need to educate ourselves about blindness/visual impairment and the abilities of blind/VI people.

Do you know many blind/VI adults? For most sighted people, experience with blindness is limited—perhaps to an acquaintance from college, a job, or the neighborhood, or even to someone standing on a city street corner selling pencils. Do you base your understanding of blindness/visual impairment on just one person? Was that person competent in the skills of blindness/visual impairment so that he or she could handle the activities of life—school, a job, a household, a family—efficiently and independently?

Blind/VI people are a cross section of humanity. There is no *blind personality,* no *psychology of blindness.* If you meet a group of blind/VI people, you will find just as much variation in personality, interests, and talents as in a group of sighted people. There are tall ones, short ones, bright ones, not-so-bright ones, kind ones, obnoxious ones, extraordinary people and ordinary ones, just like you or me, who go about their business, leading regular lives—going to work, raising a family, cooking their meals, taking care of their homes, solving problems, volunteering in the community, enjoying hobbies, having fun.

Becoming acquainted in person or through reading with competent, successful blind/VI adults is one way to develop positive attitudes about blindness and the abilities of blind/VI people.

Dr. Abraham Nemeth

Consider the story of Abraham Nemeth. Dr. Nemeth is the creator of the Nemeth Code for Braille Mathematics. Blind from birth, Dr. Nemeth grew up in New York City where he traveled the buses and subways of that metropolis independently. He went on to study at Columbia University and earned two doctorate degrees, one in psychology and one in mathematics. During his 30 years as a professor, Dr. Nemeth taught a variety of undergraduate mathematics courses and graduate courses in computer science such as systems programming, automata theory, and artificial intelligence. To this day, Dr. Nemeth remains involved in research and computer science.

Dr. Nemeth says that he was discouraged from making mathematics his undergraduate major by vocational counselors because of his blindness and the lack of braille materials. He acquiesced and switched to psychology instead. But take a look at the courses he chose for his electives at college—analytic geometry, differential and integral calculus, modern geometry, statistics—any math courses he could get his hands on. Dr. Nemeth reports that his counselors were correct that there were no braille materials for mathematics at that level, so he created them himself! The code that Dr. Nemeth invented in order to complete his college courses in time became the official code in which all mathematics notation is written for blind people in the United States and other countries. Dr. Nemeth writes:

> I hope that [my] experience ... demonstrates how important are the early acquisitions of braille skills, facility in mobility, a knowledge of print practice, and good attitudes. Equipped with these skills, a blind person can progress as far as his motivation, his ingenuity, and his talent will permit. Without them, a blind person is restricted to semi-literacy and lack of independence. (Nemeth, 1992)

Dr. Geerat Vermeij

Have you read about Geerat Vermeij? Dr. Vermeij developed a love of nature as a young child and knew by age 10 that he wanted to become a biologist. He, too, was discouraged from his desired path by vocational counselors who felt that a science that depended so much on observation could not possibly be a fitting occupation for a blind person. These counselors were acting on the mistaken belief that observation was solely a visual skill. In spite of the warnings, Dr. Vermeij went on to study at Princeton and Yale and became one of the preeminent scientists in the field. His teaching and research interests include the coevolutionary reactions between predators and prey and their effects on morphology, ecology, and evolution; and the paleobiogeography of the Arctic and its influence on Atlantic and Pacific Cenozoic fauna. His life and work have been featured in magazines and a PBS television series. Dr. Vermeij states:

In short, there is nothing about my job that makes it unsuitable for a blind person. Of course, there are inherent risks in the field work; I have been stung by rays, bitten by crabs, and detained by police who mistook my partner and me for operatives trying to overthrow the government of their African country, and I have slipped on rocks, scraped my hand on sharp oysters and pinnacles of coral, and suffered from stomach cramps. There isn't a field scientist alive or dead who hasn't had similar experiences. Life without risk is life without challenge; one cannot hope to understand nature without experiencing it firsthand. (Vermeij, 1994, p. 81)

POSSIBILITIES

Of course, not every blind/VI person will go to a prestigious university and rise to the top of his or her field. Blind/VI students run the gamut from those with cognitive disabilities to those who are geniuses, just as sighted students do. The experiences of Dr. Vermeij and Dr. Nemeth, however, demonstrate that blindness/visual impairment does not need to stop anyone from achieving academic and life success. Blind/VI students can take the most rigorous courses in high school and attend college and graduate school in the most demanding disciplines. Blindness/visual impairment does not impose limits on what a person can learn or what area he or she can study. What might limit a blind/VI person are the same things that might limit anyone— interests, talents, IQ, ambition, none of which is related to blindness. Blindness/visual impairment need not stop a person from excelling at academics, accomplishing goals, and fulfilling dreams. The key is to have appropriate expectations from the start, so that the young blind/VI student is introduced to academic work on the same schedule as sighted students of comparable ability. Having materials in accessible form is another necessity, and, of course, making sure the student is taught the skills and tools needed to handle the work.

At conferences of the National Federation of the Blind, the largest organization of blind/VI people in the nation, I have met a blind mathematician, lawyer, college professor, chemist, industrial arts teacher, elementary school teacher, National Aeronautics and Space Administration engineer, physician, chef, bee keeper, car body mechanic, transmission mechanic, Foreign Service Officer, triathlete, and a sailor who sailed solo from San Francisco to Hawaii. Twice. In a race. And came in third. Not to mention the blind man who climbed the highest peaks on every continent and, in May of 2001, reached the summit of Mount Everest!

So, does blindness mean helplessness and limitations? We can make it mean that. Without even realizing it, we can limit our blind/VI students because of beliefs we may hold about the limitations blindness imposes.

But it's far better for the child if we make blindness mean *possibilities* instead. The adults in the blind/VI child's life—teachers, administrators, IEP team, parents—need to keep the doors of opportunity open. We need to have expectations for the blind/VI student based on cognitive ability, not based on blindness/visual impairment. We need to question our assumptions. We need to provide fair evaluations, accessible materials, and good education and training. We need to stop thinking *limits* and start thinking *possibilities*.

The Can't-Do Approach	The Can-Do Approach
Helpless	Can learn skills
Pity	It's okay to be blind/VI
Can't learn	Needs appropriate materials
A loss	A difference
Limitations	Possibilities

The job of the blind/VI child sometimes seems huge to sighted people—we just can't imagine being able to do things without our eyesight. But I think the kids take it in stride. Life as a blind person need not be any more frustrating or stressful than life with eyesight—*as long as blind/VI children are taught the skills and given the tools they need* to accomplish tasks with independence and with success. If the adults in the child's life have positive attitudes about blindness and the abilities of blind/VI people and a basic understanding of the skills the child is learning, they can help move the child along and bring the day of independence closer and closer.

CHAPTER 3

A SKILLS DEFINITION OF BLINDNESS

The dictionary defines blindness as lacking or extremely deficient in the ability to see. The law defines blindness as a visual acuity of 20/200 or less in the better eye with corrective lenses or a visual field of 20 degrees or less in the better eye. The IDEA defines visual impairment and blindness as an impairment in vision which, even after correction, adversely affects educational performance. Rehabilitation counselors refer to an inability to read ordinary newsprint, even with the best correction. Low vision. Partially sighted. Visually impaired. Legally blind. What does it all mean?

The use of the word *blind* often causes confusion and sometimes even controversy. Some in the field of blindness/visual impairment use the word blind to include the whole range of visual impairment; others do the opposite, using the term *visual impairment* to include blindness. Some make marked distinctions among the various levels of eyesight; others prefer to merge them into one. Members of the general public, who usually think of blindness as not being able to see, are often surprised to learn that most people who are considered blind for legal and educational purposes actually have some vision. In fact, only about 10% of blind people are totally or almost totally blind.

Making It Work: Educating the Blind/VI Student in the Regular School, 15–22
Copyright © 2005 by Information Age Publishing

THE SKILLS DEFINITION

I'd like to propose a way of defining blindness/visual impairment that is not based on deficiencies, limitations, or things that a person *can't* do. I propose that blindness/visual impairment simply means *using alternative skills and tools in place of, or in addition to, eyesight in order to gain information or perform tasks.*

So if the task is cleaning the kitchen counter, the skill might be wiping the counter using a pattern of vertical and horizontal strokes to make sure the whole area is covered. If the task is sorting laundry, the tool might be braille or tactile labels. If the job is taking notes at a Parent Teacher Association meeting, the skill might be using a slate and stylus or electronic notetaker. If the errand is going into town to make a purchase, the skill might be walking with a cane or guide dog, using public transportation, or hiring a driver.

The same types of options exist for school-related tasks. If the task is reading, the alternative tool might be braille or large print. If it's coloring a Thanksgiving cornucopia, the tools might be scented markers or crayons, a raised-line drawing, and a coloring screen (see page 155). If the task is learning multiplication, the tool might be manipulatives coded with feelable textures. If students need to report on a newspaper article, the skill might be using a reader, finding an article online, or calling NFB Newsline. Just about any school task you can think of can be done by the blind/VI student who has been taught the skill to do it.

Being blind/visually impaired doesn't mean that a student can't do things. It certainly doesn't mean that he or she will have an adverse educational outcome. It does mean the student will need to learn alternative skills. Don't get hung up on whether the student should be labeled blind or visually impaired. Think instead about *whether the student has the skills needed to do the job.*

A BLINDNESS SKILLS QUIZ

One of the most important skills of blindness/visual impairment is being creative in devising ways to accomplish tasks that sighted people usually do with eyesight. See if you can think of simple, practical ways that blind/VI people might accomplish the following common tasks.

How might a blind/visually impaired person...?

    ... keep track of where his/her toddler is?
    ... shop at the supermarket?

... grill meat on a barbecue?
... go on the Internet?
... get to work?
... locate a certain office in a new building?
... pour a glass of juice?
... iron a shirt?
... mow the lawn?

Here are some possible solutions.

- To keep track of a toddler, a blind/VI parent might attach bells to the baby's shoes (as many sighted parents do) or pay attention to the rustle of plastic diapers.
- To shop, a blind/VI person might write a shopping list in braille, make use of the store's courtesy service, ask a reader or driver to come along to assist, or shop online.
- To use a grill, many blind/VI people use long oven mitts and a grilling basket.
- To go on the Internet, a blind/VI person might use a screen enlarging program or a screen reading program that makes the computer talk.
- To get to work a blind/VI person might walk, take public transportation, or get a ride with a colleague, perhaps offering to pay for gas in exchange.
- To pour, some blind/VI people use the sound of the liquid and the weight of the glass to tell when the glass is getting full, or hook one finger over the edge of the glass and stop pouring when the liquid reaches their finger.
- To iron, a blind/VI person might place the different areas of the garment on the ironing board in a systematic way and check for wrinkles by touch.
- To mow a lawn, a blind/VI person might use a systematic pattern, first mowing up and down the lawn and then across or perhaps moving in concentric squares.

These are only a few of the possible solutions for the tasks above. Blind/VI people use an array of skills and tools to successfully accomplish the tasks of life—at home, at school, in the workplace, and in the community. Some of the skills and systems are taught to them by specialists (for example, braille) and some they devise themselves. The tools they use range from regular off-the-shelf items to special devices designed specifically for blind/VI people.

So the question for school personnel becomes not *can* my student accomplish this task, but *what method and materials will my student use* to accomplish this task? The teacher of the visually impaired (TVI) will do the actual teaching of the various tools and techniques, but if classroom teachers understand the process and can envision the possibilities, then the student will be included in every activity and will be well on his/her way to becoming a skilled, competent person.

In the early grades, it is up to the adults in the child's life to make sure that the student is taught the different techniques and exposed to the various options. Instill in the student the idea of being creative and figuring out ways to accomplish tasks and begin training him/her in how to decide which technique is appropriate for which task. A child who is familiar with the techniques and options will, as he/she gets older, be able to take on the decision making and will be accustomed to devising solutions when new situations demand it.

THE CASE FOR SKILLS

A 5-year-old boy's face is almost in his dish as he eats his lunch. He is using his partial sight to find his food.

The father of a partially sighted girl is surprised to learn that a totally blind child is doing well in a regular classroom situation. His daughter is in a special ed classroom, though she is very intelligent and has no learning problems or delays. She simply cannot keep up with the pace of reading in the regular class. She reads print, but she can only read it when it is extremely enlarged on a closed circuit television.

The mother of a 7-year-old partially sighted boy doesn't quite believe it when she hears that a totally blind seven-year-old is crossing quiet streets independently. "If my child can't do it, how can a totally blind child do it?" she asks.

"My child isn't blind. She doesn't need braille." But when the partially sighted youngster reaches second grade, her mother realizes the child cannot read at all. By the time braille instruction is finally initiated, the student is lagging far behind her classmates. "I had been so happy that my daughter 'wasn't blind.' Now I see that braille is not a curse of blindness, but a tool of literacy and freedom," the mom says.

"My son doesn't need a cane. He gets around fine. He's not blind; he's visually impaired." Yet when asked if the child is comfortable walking in unfamiliar areas, the mom replies that in such situations, they always hold hands. Holding hands with a child is very nice, but is this holding hands because you want *to or because you* have *to? And is it still appropriate when the child is 11, 12, 13 years old?*

What do these stories have in common? It is the fact that no one taught these partially sighted children the skills that would enable them to get the job done in an efficient, safe, effective manner. After all, these children were not *blind*.

Who Is Blind?

Some professionals in the blindness/visual impairment field insist on a strict distinction being made between those who are totally or almost totally blind and those who have some sight. They prefer that the word *blind* be used only for the first group and another term like *visually impaired* or *low vision* be used to refer to people who have some remaining eyesight. In their view it is not only reasonable, but accurate to categorize based on how much eyesight a person has.

Although at first glance this categorization might make sense, there are serious problems with it. When we examine the premises of this position we discover that the beliefs and assumptions underlying it actually work to the detriment—not the benefit—of those being categorized. Let's take a look at some of these assumptions.

The first assumption is that there are real and profound differences between visually impaired and totally blind people—in their needs, their abilities, their perceptions, their potential.

The next assumption is that it is inherently better to be partially sighted than to be totally blind. In this view the visually impaired have an advantage over those without eyesight. Eyesight in and of itself is held to be the basis of this superiority. In this belief system, the more eyesight a person has, the better off he or she is bound to be—more able, more independent, more successful.

In this view, there is a neat division of skills and techniques: the visually impaired can use visual (superior) techniques, while the blind *have to* use tactile (inferior) techniques. Visually impaired people use print; blind people have to use braille. Visually impaired people use eyesight to get around; blind people need travel aids like canes or dogs. In this view, the use of these skills is negative, defeating, inferior. The use of these skills means the person is blind and of course, blindness is what must be avoided at all costs.

It follows, then, that we would not want to make someone blind by using the term *blind* for people who have some eyesight. It is said, after all, that the public fears blindness almost as much as they fear cancer and AIDS, and people seem to want to avoid the word. Likewise, we would not want to make someone blind by having him/her use the skills of blindness.

Damaging Results

Damaging results stem from this rigid categorization by level of eyesight and the set of assumptions that underlie it. First, people with partial sight are kept from learning skills that would help them in their daily lives, indeed, that would enable them to lead independent lives. Using solely visual skills can actually render a person helpless. For example, if the environment changes—if it becomes dark or if the terrain becomes uneven—the visually impaired person who possesses visual skills alone might be at a complete loss. The person who also possesses nonvisual skills, however, is free and competent in all situations.

It is illogical to ask people to rely solely on the sense that is impaired, instead of using the senses that are fully working, or pairing those senses with the partial sight. Why rely solely on impaired vision when adding other methods would ensure that the person got the whole picture?

The misguided effort to have partially sighted people appear sighted—and, by extension, *normal*—ends up depriving them of the very things they need to be functional. So, ironically, while partially sighted children are using only visual techniques and must put their faces in their bowls to find their food, hold hands with their mothers, and be placed in special classes, their "blinder" counterparts are learning skills that enable them to eat gracefully, travel in unfamiliar places, cross streets safely and age appropriately, and keep up in class.

Another damaging result of this misguided thinking can be a sense of inferiority or even shame on the part of the partially sighted person. From a very young age, partially sighted children receive the message that the adults in their lives are very pleased when the children use their eyesight for a task. They are constantly asked, "Can you see this?" and they quickly learn that if they see something with their eyes, it is a cause for celebration; likewise, if they can't, it is a disappointment to the people most important to them.

Unfortunately, partially sighted children also learn that if being able to see something visually is superior to not being able, then full eyesight must be superior to partial eyesight. At some point they realize they cannot do things visually as well as fully sighted people, yet they are continually asked and expected to do just that. Many children have eyesight that changes; it might work well one day but poorly the next. Others lose their ability to function visually when the lighting changes, for example, when they step outdoors. Others cannot see at all at night. With so much emphasis placed on the use of the impaired sight, the partially sighted person is bound to come out feeling on the inferior side of things.

Another aspect of the visual skills only model that hurts children is the fact that many blind/VI children use the eyesight that they have very, very well. Parents and teachers are usually relieved by this, saying, "She uses her sight so well" or "He doesn't need braille or large print or a cane. Look at how well he does this or does that." But the fact is that these children still have vision impaired enough for them to be eligible for special education and other services. Should we really be encouraging (or forcing) them to use only visual techniques or offering them only materials meant to be accessed by those with normal eyesight? Is this not pushing the use of visual skills beyond the point of efficiency, beyond comfort, beyond common sense?

Partially sighted children are not in a position to realize that they are being deprived of the very skills that would enable them to compete. The visual skills only model does not have answers for the child who cannot copy quickly from the blackboard, cannot read his/her own notes, and cannot tell the difference between a shadow and a drop-off and ends up tripping down a curb on a school field trip. Parents and teachers usually don't realize either that the child needs alternative skills, and alas, everyone blames the whole problem on the visual impairment, believing that the visual impairment—and not the lack of skills—is responsible for the problems the child is having.

SKILLS GET THE JOB DONE

So, how logical is it to categorize people by how much eyesight they have if it keeps the skills and tools they need out of their hands? Does the use of nonvisual skills *make a person blind* or does it instead give a person the chance to gain competence, feel confident, be efficient, and look relaxed and graceful as he/she goes about daily life? Using the nonvisual skills doesn't make a person look blind; it makes a person look competent! Using nonvisual skills doesn't deprive people of the visual world; it adds the enriching perceptions of the other senses.

The skills definition of blindness/visual impairment avoids all the confusion about who is blind and who is not and removes the emotion from the discussion. It takes the emphasis off eyesight and puts it on the task at hand. It doesn't care whether the person is considered blind or visually impaired. It simply asks *does the person have the skills to get the job done?*

There is no negative to having an extra skill or tool in your toolbox. One progressive orientation & mobility (O&M) instructor often says "Use your eyesight for what you can see and the skills of blindness for what you can't see."[1] The integration of nonvisual skills with the person's eyesight, when the eyesight is reliable, is what will lead to the efficient, timely, safe, and graceful completion of tasks.

The blind/VI person should feel free to choose among the whole array of possible techniques in order to accomplish a task. What is the job? If the job is reading, and the visually impaired student cannot keep up with the class because impaired vision does not allow him/her to read print in the quantities and at the speed necessary to keep up with the class, *then give that student braille!* If the job is walking along with the class on a field trip and the child's impaired vision keeps him/her from seeing curbs and steps, *then put a cane in that child's hand!* If the job is eating a bowl of soup, and the visually impaired child is practically putting his/her face into the bowl to see the food, *teach that child the nonvisual method* so that he/she can look graceful and normal at the lunch table!

Assume that a blind/VI person can accomplish the task (remember the blind biologist, the sailor, the mountain climber, the chef). Next, observe the child and analyze the task. If the child is using only visual techniques, see if the job is getting done efficiently and in a timely manner. If you determine that eyesight alone is not efficient for the task, provide the alternative nonvisual skills and tools that are needed. Blind/VI people and TVIs have worked out methods for most tasks. Many times you and your student will be able to figure out simple, efficient methods on your own.

One last note about skills. Research has shown that partially sighted high school students who received braille training in the early grades 4 to 5 days a week achieved literacy levels on a par with or above sighted peers. Partially sighted students who received less braille training, began braille training later, *or relied only on print and optical aids* posted scores significantly lower than their sighted and early braille-learning peers (Ryles, 2000). Other research has revealed that although the percentage of unemployed blind/VI people is very high, of those blind/VI people who are employed, 85% read braille (Ryles, 2000, p. 472).

So don't deprive your student—make sure he/she learns the skills that will lead to full literacy, full participation in class, freedom of movement, and future employment.

NOTE

1.   I first heard Joe Cutter use a version of this statement in a presentation at the Seminar of the National Organization of Parents of Blind Children during the 1994 National Convention of the National Federation of the Blind. He attributes the statement to an unnamed parent.

CHAPTER 4

THE SKILLS AND TOOLS OF BLINDNESS

The skills and tools of blindness/visual impairment enable the student to perform the range of tasks expected of him or her in school. These skills and tools are taught to the student by specialists in the field. Speak with your student, the teacher of the visually impaired (TVI), and the family to find out which tools and techniques will work best for your student. This chapter will provide an overview of these specialized skills and tools.

The young student—preschool, kindergarten, and primary levels—will still be in the process of learning the skills and tools and finding out which works best for each task. The older student—around fourth grade and up—will have more independence in knowing what works best and deciding which tools and techniques to use.

READING AND WRITING

Reading demands can be heavy in school, as they are in the world of work in our information-rich society. The blind/visually impaired student must have good literacy skills in order to handle the flow of information. Here are some specifics:

- The student needs an efficient, reliable reading and writing medium that enables the student to handle the amount of reading

Making It Work: Educating the Blind/VI Student in the Regular School, 23–43
Copyright © 2005 by Information Age Publishing

required and to read it at a fast enough pace to keep up with the
class.

- The reading medium should allow the child to read for an
extended time without discomfort, postural strain, or undue
fatigue.

- The medium should enable the student to read fast enough to com-
prehend, and to learn spelling, grammar, capitalization, punctuation, and other literacy skills.

- The medium should be flexible so that the student can read and
write under various circumstances. For example, he/she should be
able to read in the classroom, in the library, in bed at night; he/she
should be able to take notes at a meeting or during a science lab
conducted in a darkened room or outside.

- The medium must enable the student to take *and read back* his/her
own notes. *Other people should not be taking notes for the blind/VI student!* Notetaking not only serves to record information, but also
serves as a learning tool, assisting the student in comprehending
the material. The thinking skills required in notetaking—such as
deciding what should be written down, what should get emphasis,
and so forth—are as absolutely necessary for the blind/VI student to
learn as they are for any other student.

- Last but not least, the reading medium should enable the student
to read for pleasure.

Print and/or Braille?

For a variety of reasons, the teaching of braille to blind/VI students has
waned since the 1960s. For example, in 1963, 57% of blind/VI students
knew braille; by 1998, that percentage had dropped to less than 10%
(Ryles 2000, p. 463). It's easier to teach print to partially sighted students
than to teach braille—it takes less time; classroom teachers already know
it; all you have to do is enlarge things. And teaching print seems to offer
benefits—after all, it's a print world, isn't it?

But do the supposed advantages of print actually benefit the student?
This is a serious question because many print-reading partially sighted
students do not reach the same literacy levels as their fully sighted peers.
Braille-reading students, on the other hand, attain literacy levels equal to
and sometimes above those of sighted students (see page 22). Students
who are denied braille often cannot effectively complete advanced classes
in world languages, math, and the sciences. And since the braille literacy
issue extends to life beyond school (remember that of those blind/VI peo-

ple who are employed, 85% are braille readers), by not teaching braille to partially sighted students, educators could be denying them entry into satisfying jobs and careers.

Picture a child who can only read print when the letters are highly magnified on a closed-circuit television (CCTV); imagine a student who must take frequent breaks due to eyestrain and postural fatigue; picture a student who must spend considerable time struggling to find and focus on words on the blackboard with a telescope. Chances are these children will not develop the same literacy levels as their classmates. They may also never read a book for pleasure. (Would you be tempted to read *War and Peace* on a computer screen with letters four inches high?) If you want your student to want to read, give him/her a workable medium.

It is very possible that the students described above should continue to learn print, but with the addition of braille. Likewise, recorded books are fine for limited reading tasks, but they do not teach or reinforce literacy skills and should not be a child's primary reading medium.

Literacy skills and job prospects are two compelling reasons for teaching braille to blind/VI students; the third reason is the law. Every blind/VI child has the right to learn braille! The student's future need for the medium must be considered before braille can be ruled out. (Please see Reading and Writing Medium/a, page 53.) Think of the future. Do you expect your student to go to college? Will the student have the thinking skills that develop with note-taking practice? Will the student have the ability to take notes in circumstances such as a darkened lecture hall? (Though you may hear that blind/VI students can tape record lectures, this method is not really viable. First of all, it takes too much time; in addition to reading the assignments, the student must also listen to lectures again in their entirety in order to study. Second, the student misses the benefits of the note-taking process itself—selecting, organizing, and beginning to analyze and synthesize information.) Make sure your student is given the opportunity to learn the skills necessary to do the job.

A Variety of Skills

Whether a student uses braille, print, or both, he or she will also make use of several other reading tools and techniques such as computer enlargement and/or computer speech, a scan-and-read system, recorded and electronic books, and live readers. For information on the first three items, see the chapter on technology, page 16. For information on readers, refer to Using Readers, on page 35 of this chapter.

Print Reading

Many blind/VI students are print readers. Some use regular-size print with and without magnifiers; others use large print. Large print users need regular print copies of their textbooks, too. Words can get cut off in the enlarging process; enlarged books are in black-and-white and some assignments require the original color; assignments having to do with scale and measurement work better with regular print and a magnifier.

Useful items for students who read print (or who read both print and braille) might include the following:

- A book stand (holds the book in a position to make for comfortable reading and less postural fatigue);
- A colored acetate sheet placed over the page to be read (darkens print and increases contrast);
- Special lighting (increased or decreased);
- Reading window guide (shows only a portion of the page at one time);
- Nonglare paper;
- Bold-line paper;
- Felt-tip markers;
- Small magnifier for close-up tasks;
- Small telescope for distance tasks;
- CCTV or video magnifier; and
- Computer with screen enlargement and speech.

How the Blind/VI Student Writes

The most important consideration is for the blind/VI student to have a writing medium that enables him/her to take notes and read them back. In addition, the writing medium should enable the student to write under various lighting and other conditions and in a variety of places, for example, in different areas of the classroom or outdoors during a lab. A variety of writing implements exist for your student's use; under the TVI's guidance, he or she will learn to choose the most practical tool for the task at hand:

- Felt-tip pens
- Heavy-lined paper

Figure 4.1.   Braillewriter.

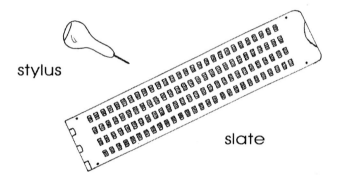

Figure 4.2.   Slate and stylus.

- Braillewriter—something like a manual typewriter, but with only six keys (all characters in braille are formed by combinations of these six keys; see Figure 4.1); younger braille users use the braille-writer for all school tasks; older students generally switch to an electronic notetaker (see Figure 4.3) except for math and some-times science. Braillewriters can be manual or electronic.
- Slate and stylus—a small, light, portable, low-tech device for pro-ducing braille; the student places the paper inside a frame (the slate) then presses the stylus to form the braille dots (see Figure 4.2).
- Electronic notetaker—a small, portable, talking computer that takes the place of a paper notebook (see Figure 4.3). The student can create folders and files for each subject. For English class, for example, the student might create files for English notes, English

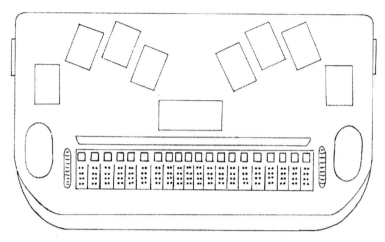

Figure 4.3.   Electronic notetaker.

homework, and English research paper. Notetakers come equipped with either a QWERTY (typewriter) or braille keyboard (six keys and a spacebar) and can have a braille display. The speech can be turned on and off and can be accessed with earphones. Notetakers can be connected to printers to produce print and braille copies of the student's work. (See Technology, page 163, for more details.)

- Computer—a computer can be equipped with speech, braille, and screen magnification software. Students who cannot see the screen at all do not use the mouse, but instead operate the computer using keyboard commands and speech or braille output. Earphones can be connected for quiet use. The blind/VI student can use a computer for word-processing tasks, email, going online, and so forth.
- The student might use a closed circuit television or video magnifier for certain writing tasks.

Braille Reading

Braille is simply another way of writing the alphabet. Braille reading and writing are the equivalent of print reading and writing. The braille user will read and learn the same things using braille that the sighted children in your class read and learn using print. Anything that is written in print can be written in braille, including algebra, chemistry, music, and world languages.

Eliminating "the Braille Gap"

It's important for teachers who have a braille user in the classroom to use techniques that will eliminate the braille gap, a situation in which the teacher has no idea of the child's work. This situation can occur if the student's braille work is not transcribed into print. For example, if the students journal every day, the blind/VI student might produce several pages of writing each week. If this work is not transcribed into print, the teacher will have no idea of what the child is writing about and will have a difficult time judging his/her progress. Here are some ideas for eliminating the braille gap:

* Become familiar with the basics of braille.
* Ask the TVI for a braille cheat sheet, an alphabetical listing of the braille letters, contractions, and punctuation marks.
* If the student's work has not been transcribed into print, ask the child to read what he/she wrote to you.
* A classroom aide who is assisting a braille user should be learning braille; eventually, he/she will be able to write in the print on the child's braille work. *But aides new to braille make mistakes!* Make sure the child is not marked wrong for mistakes the aide made. Ask the TVI to check the print transcription until the aide's skills are up to snuff.
* Ask the TVI about technology that can provide you with a printout of the student's work.

A Quick Braille Lesson

The basic unit in braille is the braille cell. A braille cell is made up of six possible dots, arranged in two columns of three dots each, and numbered one to six (see Figure 4.4).

Braille letters and other symbols are formed by using one or more of the six dots. For example, dot 1 is the letter a. Dots 1 and 2 form the letter b. Sometimes two cells are used in combination. Upper case letters,

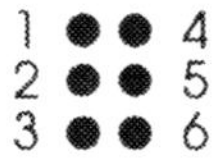

```
1 ● ● 4
2 ● ● 5
3 ● ● 6
```

Figure 4.4.   The Braille cell.

Figure 4.5.   Lowercase and capital letters.

for example, are formed by writing dot 6 (the capital sign) followed by the letter (Figure 4.5).

First children learn the alphabet in braille (see Figure 4.6). After that, they begin learning the braille contractions. In braille, contractions are used to save space and to make reading and writing faster. For example, the word *braille* is written *brl*. Contractions are usually taught right after the child learns the alphabet because almost all the reading material the braille student will encounter will be written in contracted braille. Uncontracted braille (also called Grade 1 Braille) might be found in phonics or spelling books, but for the most part, books are transcribed in contracted (also called Grade 2) braille. (The terms *Grade 1 Braille* and *Grade 2 Braille* refer only to whether or not the braille is contracted and do not refer to the grade the student is in when learning the different levels of braille.)

When a student learns to read in a regular classroom, he/she usually learns the braille contractions as they occur in the classroom reading material.

The student will also learn punctuation in braille. Braille punctuation marks are shaped like letters, but are formed in the lower part of the cell, using only dots 2, 3, 5, and 6.

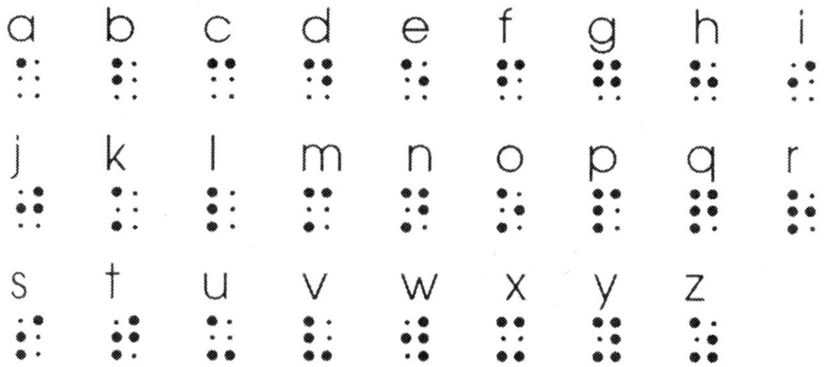

Figure 4.6.   The Braille alphabet.

Find the one that is different.

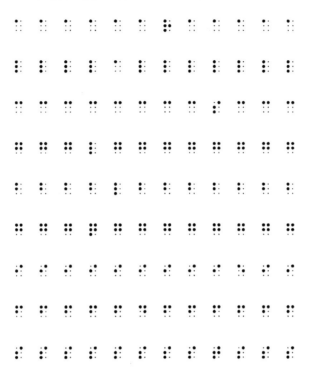

Figure 4.7.   Worksheet.

Try It Out

Figures 4.7 and 4.8 are two braille worksheets, similar to the kind beginning braille students might be given (of course, theirs would have real raised dots). Follow the instructions and see how quickly you can learn the basics of braille. Incidentally, sighted people usually read braille with their eyes.

Did you notice that the differences became slightly more difficult to discern as the lines went on? Hopefully you were still able to differentiate. Braille does contain a few letters that look similar, just as print does. The letters that are confusables in braille, however, are not the same ones that are easily confused in print. For example, while *b* and *d* are typical print reversals, *f* and *d* would be typical reversals in braille. It is helpful for classroom teachers to know this, so that they do not think that their young braille user does not know the letter sounds!

Find the one that matches the first one on each line.

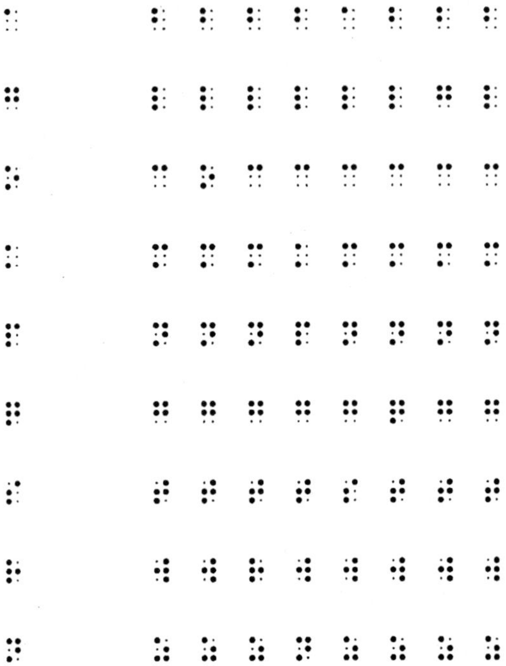

Figure 4.8.   Worksheet

Next, using the following four letters, see if you can read these simple words.

a   b   c   l   t

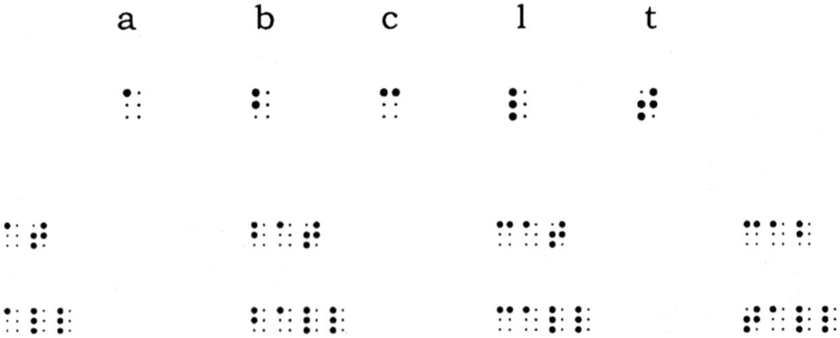

Can you read these simple words?

Braille Reading Technique

Braille is read with the wrists raised and the fingers rounded so that the fingertip pads touch the dots. Braille characters are recognized by their total shape, not by their individual dots. In order to perceive the shape of the dots, light movement across the dots is needed. Good reading technique involves putting as many fingers of both hands as possible on the line of braille. Fast braille readers read using a sort of zigzag movement across and down the lines of braille. Ask your student's TVI or a blind adult to demonstrate good technique.

Writing in Braille

Braille reading and writing are usually taught together. As students learn to recognize each letter by its shape, they also learn how to write each letter by its dot numbers. Students generally learn how to write braille on a braillewriter. Each of the braillewriter's six keys corresponds to one of the six dots of the braille cell. Keys are pressed one at a time or in combination to form each letter or other symbol. Students also learn how to write braille using a slate and stylus. Writing on a slate begins at the right edge of the paper. The paper is turned over to read the braille.

High-tech devices are also used for writing braille. Please see the technology chapter, page 161, and How the Blind/VI Student Writes, page 26.

Braille Numbers

The first 10 letters of the braille alphabet also serve as numbers, when written after a symbol called the number sign. Numbers written in this manner are called literary numbers, since they are formed from literary braille, the braille that is used in books.

When a child begins to learn math, he/she is taught to read and write numbers in Nemeth Code, the system for writing math in braille. In Nemeth Code, the shapes of the numbers are the same as their literary counterparts, but they are formed in the lower part of the cell, using only dots 2, 3, 5, and 6 (see Figure 4.9).

The Nemeth Code allows for all mathematical expressions to be written in braille, from simple addition and subtraction to algebraic equations and scientific notation.

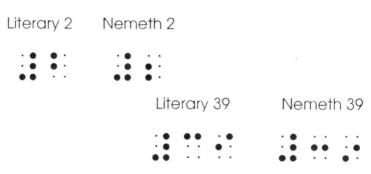

Figure 4.9.   Numbers in Braille.

For further information on reading and writing braille and using braille in the classroom, see *The Bridge to Braille: Reading and School Success for the Young Blind Child* (Castellano & Kosman, 1997) and other books listed in Resources, page 209.

INTERPRETING TACTILE GRAPHICS

Because most braille volumes do not contain illustrations, blind/VI children often get little practice in interpreting tactile graphics. Added to the lack of tactile illustrations is the fact that there is little standardization governing the creation of these graphics. Although the ability to glean information from illustrations is crucial for many school subjects, many blind/VI children do not receive systematic instruction in this area. Classroom teachers therefore may encounter some students who are skilled at interpreting tactile graphics and many who are not.

It is only after a great deal of experience with real objects and good three-dimensional models that a young blind/VI child can begin to learn effectively from two-dimensional tactile illustrations. Learning how to decipher and interpret tactile illustrations is a process and students need to experience well-made simple drawings in the early grades so that they can decipher more complicated ones later. Students need to be shown the relationship of the 2-D drawing to the 3-D object. Tactile illustrations must be crafted so that they work well when examined by touch (see Tactile Illustrations, page 151).

Give your student lots of experience with tactile maps, charts, and graphs and be sure to teach, give practice, and test on the same illustrations so that your student will get a consistent presentation of the various concepts (please see Inconsistent Presentation, page 107). The TVI will teach a method for examining and interpreting tactile illustrations, such as scanning the outer limits of a drawing to get a sense of its size and scope and then exploring the illustration in a systematic fashion. Encourage your student to keep wrists raised as he/she examines the drawing; don't push or pull his/her hands over the drawing. A student with good skills in interpreting tactile illustrations will have success in geometry class and on college entrance tests later in life.

USING READERS

A reader is someone who reads print material directly to a blind/VI person or records it on tape for later use. The ability to use a reader effectively is one of the most important skills the blind/VI student needs to develop. Blind/VI adults use readers on the job and in their homes for personal mail and other material. Students use readers for various tasks, such as research in a library, accessing texts and articles that are not available in an accessible medium, and often in testing situations. A student's need for readers increases in the higher grades and in college. A reader can be either paid or volunteer.

Basically, a reader serves as a pair of eyes. If you think about how you might go about performing a certain reading task for yourself, you can understand how a reader operates. If you were looking through a book for a piece of information, for example, you might quickly read through the table of contents, check a few key words in the index, skim the first few paragraphs of several chapters, and skip around, skimming for a name or particular phrase. These are the kinds of tasks that a reader does. The key, however, is that *the blind/VI person directs the reader in each of these tasks*.

The blind/VI person directing a reader makes all decisions about what is to be read. The reader must realize this. The blind/VI person moves the reader through the material, telling him or her how fast to read (as fast as possible is the usual recommendation!) and when to read straight through, stop reading, skip, skim, read captions, describe illustrations, read graphs, and so forth, as necessary to extract the information the blind/VI person wants. The reader does not find the answers or do the work for the blind/VI person. The reader does not explain what has been read or teach the material to the blind/VI person. The reader is simply the conduit for the information.

In order to direct and use a reader effectively, the blind/VI student needs to know a good deal of information. He/she must be familiar with various print page formats, headings, captions, contents, indexes, and so forth, and also with the typical elements found in charts, graphs, and diagrams. The student needs to understand the set up of dictionaries, encyclopedias, newspapers, magazines, Websites, and so on. The student also needs to know what information is contained in card catalogs (paper and computer) and library databases and understand how to search them. The student should obviously be included in all school training on library, research, and other such skills.

In addition to being able to listen well, the blind/VI student needs to learn how to quickly synthesize and analyze the material he/she is hearing in order to decide what is important and what can be skipped or skimmed. Chances are the student will be taking notes during the reading session, so notetaking skills are also of great importance.

In order to give good direction to a reader and to keep appropriate control of the reading situation, the student needs to develop social inter-action ability, communication skills, and assertiveness.

Training a student in all these skills begins with every book the child reads, every social interaction, every lesson on library skills, and every subject which requires notetaking. Most often family members are the child's first readers, but the TVI, classroom teachers, and the librarian all play a part in making sure the child gains the skills.

Training the Student to Use a Reader

The TVI begins the student's formal training in how to use a reader, but often the student also gets on the job training during school when someone reads print material that has not been enlarged or brailled or when the class visits the library to do research. The person who trains a student in using a reader usually plays two roles during the training, that of reader and that of teacher, stepping in and out of each role as needed. As reader, the person stays relatively quiet and follows the student's direction. As teacher, the person asks questions to help the student think, and gives suggestions and explanations when needed. For example, he/she might say, "Okay, I'm going to stop being your reader for a second. You know we just came to a graph. What might you want to tell your reader to do now?"

A useful way to get the student thinking about the process is to give him/her an assignment to find a certain piece of information in a book using a reader. Before you begin reading, ask the student to think about how he/she would go about trying to find that piece of information if he/she were able to access the book him/herself. The student can then try giving the reader directions based on how he/she would approach the task. Give your student some practice interrupting the reader to ask for the spelling of words or names, to tell the reader to reread a section or to skip, or to ask for a description of visual material.

One beginning training idea is to simulate real assignments but apply them to simple materials that the student is already familiar with. For example, a typical English class assignment might be the following:

> Leonora learns a lesson in the novel. Tell what lesson she learns. Support your idea with examples from the text.

Instead of using a novel that the class has read, however, use a simple book or story like "Little Red Riding Hood" or "The Three Little Pigs." The student then directs the reader to the parts of the story that have the information needed. As reader, sit quietly and await instructions from the student and then follow them exactly, whether they are good instructions or not. Through exercises like this the student will learn ways to give clear, concise direction.

Another training exercise could be to assign the student to research a certain piece of information, for example, the population of a certain country, from an encyclopedia-type article. In this exercise the student would practice instructing the reader to begin reading the article, but to skip to the next paragraph when the student says, "Skip." The idea is for the student to begin recognizing very quickly when a paragraph is likely to contain the needed information and when it does not have to be read fully.

The student will probably get real experience using a reader at the library when the first research paper is assigned. When trying to decide which books would be useful for his/her topic, the student might direct the reader first to read the table of contents, then to check the index for certain entries. He/she might ask the reader to turn to a certain chapter and read the first paragraph or the first sentence of each paragraph and to look for certain key names or words. The final decision about which books to choose should be the student's. If it is clear that the student needs more practice before he/she can make these decisions successfully, it would make sense for the reader to step out of the reader role at times to offer further tips and instruction.

One of the difficulties of training a child in reader skills in school is that the readers are usually adults and it can be awkward for a child to take charge and give direction to an adult. Likewise, sometimes the adult takes over the process. Be alert to this potential problem. If the student is being too passive, help him/her learn to be more assertive. If the adult is taking over, remind him/her that it is necessary for the blind/VI person to be in charge of the task. Possible in-school readers might be a classroom aide, a volunteer from the community, or an older student.

In college and in adult life, the blind/VI person will be responsible for hiring, training, directing, supervising, and yes, firing readers when necessary. Keep this in mind as you provide training to your student in this critical skill.

INDEPENDENT MOVEMENT AND TRAVEL

This skill area is usually referred to as orientation and mobility, or O&M for short. Orientation means knowing where you are in space and mobility refers to the ability to get where you want to go. A useful way to think about a student's need for training in the area of O&M is to consider whether or not the child is able to move about with age-appropriate independence. For children with developmental delay, this can be thought of as stage-appropriate independence.

Encourage the youngest blind/VI children to be active, moving about and exploring the environment. Active movement stimulates curiosity and interaction with the world and the people in it. This in turn leads to the development of concepts and problem-solving skills. O&M instructors can provide ideas for movement and exploration. Build in time for exploration of the classroom and other areas of the school environment.

The *independent* part of independent movement and travel is extremely important. *The student should not be led around!* In order for the child to internalize the expectation of independent movement, the adults in his/her life must believe in it and set the stage for it to happen. If you are imagining an independent future for your blind/VI student, make sure you are on the road that leads there. Constantly guiding a child from place to place *does not lead to independence*. The main guiding that adults should be doing is guiding the child to make discoveries.

Who Should Use a Cane?

If using a cane would improve the child's posture, gait, and movement and enhance confidence and safety in moving around, then that child should use a cane. Would a cane benefit a child who has some vision? Again, the question is not should a partially sighted child use a cane. The question is does this particular child have the skills and ability to move about safely and independently? If not, what skills and tools does the child need in order to do this? Observe the child's functioning indoors and outdoors; in familiar areas and unfamiliar areas; on sunny days, on overcast days, at night. Does he/she have any trouble at curbs or steps? Is he/she safe crossing streets? Does he/she have fears about moving about in new environments or when the lighting is not ideal? Is the child expending so much energy just trying to *see* that he/she has very little energy left to think about where he/she is going, have a conversation with a friend, or simply enjoy the walk? A cane can be a very freeing addition for such a person. Again, thinking about whether the student has age-appropriate freedom of movement is a good way to gauge if he/she needs additional skills and tools.

Cane Travel

The cane is held so that its tip lands about three steps in front of the feet. It is swept from side to side just slightly wider than shoulder width. Like vision, the cane gives a preview of what lies ahead and to the sides. It tells if a path is clear or if an object is in the way and locates a safe spot to place the foot. It alerts to drop-offs like curbs and enables safe negotiation of stairs up or down.

The cane is supposed to touch things as the child moves along. Touching things with the cane enables the student to identify objects such as chairs, desks, trash cans, and outdoor play equipment, and to contact or avoid them as desired.

A Developmental Process

In the past, blind/VI children were not given canes until they were older teens. Nowadays they get their canes just about as soon as they can stand up. For them, learning to use the cane is a developmental process. At first the child might play with the cane and experiment with what it can do, perhaps holding it upside down or dragging it behind him/her. He/she might hold the cane in a fist (similar to the way a young child first holds a crayon). As the child begins to realize what the cane can do, he/she will begin to hold it out in front more often and perhaps even follow the shaft of the cane down to check out an object the cane has struck. In this way the cane can facilitate exploration and discovery of the world.

Several types of canes are available—metal, fiberglass, carbon fiber, rigid, folding, telescoping. For the young child with his/her still developing motor skills, strength, and dexterity, a *longer, lightweight, rigid* cane with *a narrow grip* and *metal tip* often works best. Here is some information on cane characteristics:

- The young child usually cannot yet hold the cane in a centered position in front of his/her body and might hold it resting against his/her hip. A longer length cane (up to the child's chin or nose) can make up for this lack of technique.
- The longer length also gives an extra step before the child's body will come into contact with an object the cane has struck, thereby affording the child more reaction time.

- A lighter cane material (such as fiberglass) allows the cane to be a little longer but still lightweight. A lightweight cane is more maneuverable and less tiring for a child to hold.
- A rigid lightweight cane provides good feedback/information to the child's hand and arm.
- A metal tip provides excellent echo/sound information when the child taps it or when it strikes an object, wall, or door.

As the child continues in the developmental process and gains more and more motor control, he/she will begin to hold the cane with a more standard grip and position. Eventually, the student will hold the cane with the hand centered, sliding or tapping it with a low arc from side to side, and walking in step, with the cane tip to the right when the left foot is forward and the cane tip to the left when the right foot is forward. Learning and mastering these techniques enable the child to keep him/herself safe while walking briskly, purposefully, and gracefully from place to place.

Travel Skills for School

The O&M instructor will begin to teach the preschool and kindergarten-age blind/VI child the skills involved with school-related tasks such as locating the entrance to the school, the classroom, the bathrooms, the office, and the water fountain. The student will learn the techniques for going up and down the stairs and how to choke up for walking in line, in a confined space, or in a crowded hallway. When dexterity is developed enough, the child will learn the pencil grip, an easy, elegant technique for pulling the cane in close.

Sound is an important component of independent travel. The cane makes a different sound when tapped on different surfaces, such as carpet, tile, wood, or metal. As the child learns to differentiate among these sounds, he/she will begin to understand more about the school and its layout. For example, he/she will know when the cane has touched a classroom door or an exit door.

Sounds in the environment also enhance orientation. The student will learn to listen for characteristic indoor sounds such as the hum of the water fountain or phones ringing in the office to figure out where he/she is. Outdoor sounds such as buses idling or ropes clinking against the flagpole can also serve as orientation clues.

By listening to the sounds and echoes the cane makes when it is tapped, the child gets information about the space around him/her and, with practice, can tell how far he/she is from the wall and roughly how big a room is. The blind/VI child walking down a hallway can use hearing to tell the difference between a wall and an opening, such as a doorway or intersecting hallway. You can actually give the student directions such as "the office is the first open door on the left" or "the gym is the second opening on the right."

The O&M instructor will also help the student notice other distinctive characteristics of the building—for example, the carpeted floor in the library, the rubber mat outside the gym, the hot air from the kitchen fans. Slopes and differences in textures beneath the cane and the feet, such as tile, carpeting, concrete, and so on, will all help the student self-orient.

The student will begin to understand spatial concepts and will learn to use the cardinal directions, north, south, east, and west. He/she will begin to make a mental map that links together information about the different parts of a room or building. Memory and problem-solving skills will also develop, as will the ability to ask for information or directions when needed. The student will use all these skills to walk independently or with friends from class to class or from one area of the school to another.

The student will also learn the proper way to store the cane at the desk so that it is out of the way of others, but always at his/her fingertips.

Teachers Can Help the Process Along

Teachers can play an important role in helping the student progress in independent movement and travel skills. Here are some ideas:

- Give the student time for exploration and getting to know the different areas of the classroom. If the child knows the room, he/she will be able to move about independently in it.
- Encourage cane use, independent movement, problem solving, and self-orienting.
- Understand how the child gets information through the cane and the other senses. Speak positively about these techniques and foster an environment in which they are respected. Teach other students to respect the cane's space.
- Don't take the cane away. Don't lead the student around.
- If you notice the blind/VI student having difficulty in a particular area, contact the O&M instructor to provide more instruction. Then give the child opportunities to practice the new skills.
- Make sure the student uses the cane in the halls, cafeteria, playground, and so forth. The cane is a must during fire drills, even if someone else guides the student out. (If there were ever a real fire

and the guide and student became separated, the student must have a way to exit the building independently.)

TECHNOLOGY SKILLS

The blind/VI student will gain skill in the use of many pieces of high-tech equipment over the school years (please see the chapter on technology, page 161, for an overview of this equipment). The TVI and other specialists will train the student to use this equipment. Following is a typical sequence for the introduction of technology skills.

Primary Grades

- Keyboarding/touch typing
- Beginning computer skills using adaptive equipment (such as screen enlargement, speech, keyboard commands)
- Electronic notetaker
- Talking electronic dictionary (*after* learning to use a braille or print dictionary)
- Talking calculator
- CCTV/video magnifier

Middle School

- Computer literacy skills, including email and Internet
- Braille embosser
- Electronic books
- Recorded books on tape and/or CD

High School

- Scan-and-read system
- Download-and-read

GETTING THE JOB DONE

Blind/VI adults in just about every field you can think of—teachers, engineers, chemists, janitors, hotel clerks, lawyers, social workers, physicians, business owners, mechanics, and countless others—use the alternative skills of blindness/visual impairment every day to successfully fulfill the requirements of their positions. So, think about your student's future and keep expectations high. Begin from the position that the job can be accomplished with the appropriate training, tools, and skills.

CHAPTER 5

SETTING THE STAGE FOR SUCCESS

Essentials That Must Be in Place

What elements must be put in place in order to set the stage for learning success for a blind/visually impaired student? The essentials discussed in this chapter center around three important areas: positive attitudes, appropriate practices, and adequate specialized services.

Administrators, teachers, and other school staff who express positive, can-do attitudes create an atmosphere that will support and encourage the blind/VI student's progress. When the learning environment is furnished with accessible materials, the blind/VI student is afforded the same opportunities to participate as sighted children enjoy. This is especially important in the early school years. Good services from a teacher of the visually impaired and other specialists will ensure that the student learns the necessary specialized skills and the classroom teachers learn methods that will enable them to include the blind/VI student in all lessons and activities.

Setting the stage for learning success for the blind/VI student is a team effort and you will receive assistance and advice from your student's TVI. The planning and effort you put in will seem worthwhile when you see your blind/VI student participating fully, gaining skills, and reaching his/her developmental and educational goals.

Making It Work: Educating the Blind/VI Student in the Regular School, 45–64
Copyright © 2005 by Information Age Publishing

THE GOAL OF INDEPENDENCE

There are two overriding goals for the blind/VI student. The short-term goal is for the student **to participate fully and independently in class**. The long-term goal is for the blind/VI child **to grow up to be a competent, self-sufficient, independent adult**. Of course these are the goals we would have for any child. The goal of independence for the blind/VI student, however, needs to be explicit and kept in mind at all times, in order to ensure that the student receives the training and opportunity that he/she needs in order to reach the goal.

Independent participation will probably not occur from day one, but if you plan for it and set the stage for it, it will come to pass. Likewise, if you don't, it will not happen at all.

Full independent participation in the classroom may not be a reasonable goal for the blind/VI child with significant additional disabilities. But this child, too, deserves to be as independent as he/she can be in the classroom. Provide opportunities for this student to make choices whenever possible and to act upon the world, not always to be the one acted upon. The blind/VI student with multiple disabilities should have as much freedom of choice and movement as children with a similar learning profile who are fully sighted. (Please see The Child with Additional Disabilities: Some Considerations, page 96.)

POSITIVE ATTITUDES AND HIGH EXPECTATIONS

Positive attitudes lay the groundwork for success for the blind/VI student. Let the blind/VI student know that you welcome his/her presence and that you believe he/she belongs in your school. Don't pity your student; instead, let the student feel your warmth and pride as he/she makes progress, learns, and grows.

Perhaps the most important way for the adults in a blind/VI student's life to contribute to the student's success is to have high expectations for his/her achievement. The blind/VI student will need appropriate support as he/she learns in the regular school, but don't let this support devolve into coddling and low expectations.

Teachers and administrators who learn about successful blind/VI people will realize that independence and high achievement are possible. Until and unless they do, expectations are likely to remain low and it is well known that students can rise—or sink—to the expectations we set for them.

It is therefore critical for teachers, IEP team members, administrators, and parents to have the knowledge that high achievement is possible.

Books like *Extraordinary People with Disabilities* (Kent & Quinlin, 1996) and the Kernel Book series (see Resources, page 211) as well as contact with capable, successful blind/VI adults (perhaps in classroom visits) can provide information and inspiration. Once school staff members believe that this kind of success is possible, the next step is simply learning how to set the education program up. If high expectations are set, high achievement can follow.

So, expect your blind/VI student to do grade-level work. For the blind/VI student with learning or other disabilities, expect the same level of achievement as you would if that child were not blind/VI (please see below). Expect your student to learn from your instruction, not through an intermediary such as a classroom aide or the TVI. Expect your student to complete all work and to take part in all class activities and assignments. Expect your student to learn all academic subjects. Expect your student to take notes, do research, work in groups, participate in projects.

Expect your student to learn to move about the classroom and the school building independently. Expect your student to carry out ordinary classroom responsibilities such as watering the plants, carrying the milk tray, or transporting notes to the office. Expect your student to learn tasks that are repeated each day, such as putting homework in the homework bin or packing a backpack. Expect your student to participate appropriately in all ancillary activities, such as walking in line, buying lunch, and playing at recess.

Expect appropriate behavior. Expect your student to learn social skills. Expect your student to wait his/her turn, to raise his/her hand, to keep quiet while someone else is talking, and to answer when called on. Expect your student to handle age-appropriate self-help skills.

What If This Student Were Not Blind/Visually Impaired?

A very useful way to keep expectations appropriately high is to think about what you would expect from this student *if he/she were not blind/VI*. If this were a sighted student presenting the same cognitive ability, what would your expectations be? Would you expect the student to recognize letters? To write his/her name? To stand correctly to salute the flag? To wash his/her hands independently, throw trash in the wastebasket, use the bathroom without assistance, walk in line with the other students, do whatever the task is at hand?

If the answer is yes to questions like these, then in all likelihood the blind/VI student should be completing that task as well. Blindness/visual impairment should not be the reason that a child is not expected to participate in an activity or accomplish a task.

Troubleshooting

If your student is *not* participating at grade level, it is important to figure out why. Consider this scenario:

> Snack time is over and the children walk over to the sink and line up to wash their hands. All except the blind/VI student, that is. An aide comes over to that student and wipes his hands with a washcloth.

Why is that student not washing his hands on his own? A variety of reasons is possible. It is possible that the child is physically capable of doing the task, *but no one has taught him the skills* needed to accomplish the task. Or it is possible that the child is capable and has the necessary skills but *teachers assumed that he could not accomplish the task* and so did not give the child the opportunity to participate in the activity or task.

It is also possible that the child is *not* capable of doing the task, due to additional disabilities or delays. In this case it is important to determine if this is a temporary or permanent situation. In other words, is this a task that the child cannot accomplish *yet*, due to delays in the acquisition of certain skills? Or is this a task that the child is not expected to accomplish independently due to the presence of an additional disability or condition?

If the situation is temporary, perhaps a parent, the TVI, or a physical or occupational therapist, if one is involved, can give direction to school staff on how best to work on developing the skill so that the child will eventually be able to do the task. If the situation is expected to be permanent, then it would be appropriate to give assistance to the child or to do the task for him or her. It is very important to go through this analysis to determine why the child is not participating before deciding that the child cannot accomplish a task.

Remember that although not every blind/VI student will be capable of high academic achievement, *it is never the level of eyesight that determines—or even limits—the student's ability to achieve*. Potential to achieve for the blind/VI student stems from the same set of characteristics as it does for the sighted student—ability, special talent, interest, motivation, ambition, support at home, opportunity, any number of attributes—but never the amount of eyesight.

QUESTION YOUR ASSUMPTIONS

Question your assumptions about what your blind/VI student can and cannot do and don't always act on *assumptions* of help needed. Frequently, and certainly without intending to, sighted adults in the blind/VI child's life make decisions that *restrict the child's life* based on assumptions they

have about blindness/visual impairment. They *assume* the blind/VI child
cannot accomplish a certain task or that the child would be unsafe doing a
certain activity. Perhaps they think the child would have difficulty traveling through a crowded hallway or would be unsafe on the stairs or
wouldn't be able to carry both a lunch tray and a cane.

Sometimes sighted people think that eyesight is necessary to perform a
certain task—their common sense tells them that if they were blind/VI
they would have trouble doing the task. The result of acting on assumptions like these is that the blind/VI child is restricted—in his/her movement, in his/her progress, and ultimately in his/her development in all
areas.

Negative assumptions stem from a lack of knowledge about the ways in
which successful blind/VI people conduct their everyday lives. It is important to realize that blind/VI adults match their clothing, go to work, use
computers, stop at the grocery store, carry bags, manage the keys to their
homes and offices, climb stairs, take escalators, use public transportation,
travel through airports, and do any number of things that sighted people
might think are amazing. None of this is miraculous or amazing. Again,
the key is having skills.

So think about the working blind/VI people who accomplish all kinds
of tasks every day. Our blind/VI children need to be able to accomplish
tasks, too, so that they will be working people someday. Imagine an independent future for your student and make sure the student is on the road
that leads there. Don't let negative assumptions put a blockade in that
road.

Be Aware of Danger Areas

Several common traps lie in wait for educators regarding the blind/VI
student. Be aware of them and don't fall in!

- Restricting the child's movements: For example, not allowing the
  student to play on certain playground equipment or insisting that
  he/she be guided when walking.
- Inadvertently holding the student back from age-appropriate independence: There is a tendency to baby the blind/VI child and to
  fear for his/her safety. Make sure the student keeps learning skills
  that will enable him/her to handle the various situations of life and
  is allowed and encouraged to venture forward with increasing independence.
- Learned dependence: For example, when an aide hovers over the
  student, does tasks for the student that the student can do for him/

herself, or constantly guides the student, the student will learn dependence rather than grow toward independence.

- Inadvertently holding the student to a lower level of a skill when he/she has already learned a more sophisticated level: For example, insisting that the student touch the wall with the cane or a hand while traveling down a hallway, when he/she has already learned how to travel competently away from the wall.

- The Annie Sullivan syndrome: Thinking you are the savior of this child and have a mission to interpret the world for him or her. Verbal guidance can be good, but there is such a thing as too much. You should not be constantly warning the student about coming stairs, walls, obstacles, and so on. The student needs methods and tools that enable him/her to find these things on his/her own. The student needs to explore, discover, and develop independence. Seek the right balance.

- Acting on negative assumptions: Don't assume the child can't do a task or needs help. If you must act on assumptions, act on positive ones!

- Blaming the child or the visual impairment: If things are not going well in the classroom, don't automatically blame the child ("He/she must have a learning disability") or the blindness/visual impairment. It's a fact that many components are needed for a successful program. Check to see if they are all in place. Perhaps the classroom teachers need more training, or the materials are not really accessible, or the student needs more time from the TVI or O&M specialist.

The section Watch for These Common Danger Areas, page 136, further discusses these ideas.

Remember that so much of what the blind/VI child is able to achieve, especially in the early years, depends on the decisions and actions of the adults in his/her life, so learn to be positive and question your assumptions.

UNDERSTAND AND RESPECT THE ALTERNATIVE SKILLS

The skills and tools of blindness/visual impairment (see page 23) are what enable the blind/VI child to participate independently and competently in school and life activities. These are the skills that can get the job done and the blind/VI student cannot be expected to be successful in the academic curriculum without having learned them. In the early years, the student will be learning these skills at the same time he/she is moving through the academic curriculum. Make sure your student acquires the skills that enable him/her to keep up.

The TVI is responsible for the actual teaching of the alternative skills, but all school staff can help the student progress in them by having a general understanding of the skills and respecting them as the equivalent of those used by sighted students. Use positive language when referring to these alternative skills and tools, encourage their use, and emphasize their value. This will engender pride in learning in the child and will speed the process toward mastery.

GET A FAIR AND ACCURATE EVALUATION

A fair, accurate evaluation is another cornerstone of a good program for a student with a disability. Getting a fair, accurate evaluation of a blind/VI child, however, can be challenging. Very few evaluation instruments were made with blind/VI children in mind. Usually at least some test items and procedures must be modified and results can be difficult to interpret. In addition, most school personnel have not had experience testing blind/VI children and an experienced person is not always available to assist.

Evaluating the blind/VI child calls for analysis, flexibility, and interpretation. Evaluators must be able to determine whether certain test items should be included and if they can be modified. They must be able to make appropriate modifications both in test items and procedures. They must be able to judge whether answers are meaningful and results valid. For the child with additional disabilities, they must determine the sense/s through which the child best takes in information and communicates and then use those channels for testing. Again, interpreting answers and results will probably not be a straightforward process.

In addition, evaluation is another area where the blind/VI student can be vulnerable to negative preconceived notions on the part of those doing the testing. Evaluations must be free of sighted bias. If the evaluation is biased, the child's real aptitude and potential will remain hidden.

Considerations for Evaluators

- Make sure appropriate modifications to test items and procedures are made by someone with experience. The TVI is the likely person to help with this.
- Be careful not to penalize the student for test items he/she is unable to complete because of the visual impairment. Ensure that it is the

child's knowledge of the concept or skill that is being tested, not his or her ability to see.

- Be sure that test items do not require information that can only be obtained visually.

- Do not automatically omit test questions or sections based on assumptions about what blind/VI people can know and do; likewise, do not administer all parts of a test without making the necessary adaptations.

- Be flexible with scoring when portions of the test have been omitted. For example, it would not be fair to count up the number of questions answered correctly on a test and then assign a below-average score to a student who did not have the opportunity to answer all of the test questions because sections were omitted.

- Do not rely solely on test results to get a true picture of the student's levels and aptitude. Seek information from classroom teachers, parents, and others who might know the child's work and potential.

- Be aware that formatting changes and other issues can arise when tests are translated into braille or enlarged. Tests—especially parts with graphics, labels, keys, lists, columns, and long reading passages followed by questions—must be checked for accuracy and usability before the administration of the test. For example, if a graphic appears on page 27, but the caption for it appears on page 26 and the key on page 28, it might pose a problem for the student taking the test. Please see Adapting Materials, page 148.

- The same issues exist for statewide and other standardized tests. Very often, the test is available in alternative media but the practice materials are not. Obviously, this puts the blind/VI student at a disadvantage. If you create practice materials, be sure that they are adapted in the same way as the test so that the student sees how concepts will be presented and will be able to recognize them (please see Inconsistent Presentation, page 107).

- Put testing accommodations and modifications into the IEP.

Evaluation Areas

Blind/VI students are evaluated in the usual academic and developmental areas and also in areas related to blindness/visual impairment, such as braille, mobility, and the use of adaptive technology. These latter evaluations are conducted by the TVI and other specialists. The TVI might recommend a low vision evaluation administered by a low vision specialist who would make recommendations for low vision devices; and/or a functional vision assessment, administered by the TVI, which would provide information on how the child uses his/her eyesight under various conditions and circumstances. (A note about the term *functional vision*—sometimes people get the mistaken impression from this term that the vision is what makes the person functional and that the less vision the person has, the less the person is able to function. This is incorrect! The term simply refers to *how the vision functions* or *to what uses the person is able to put the vision in his/her daily functions*. If the vision is not functioning effectively, the person would simply learn nonvisual ways of accomplishing the tasks.)

The American Printing House for the Blind is a source for some testing materials in adapted form. Please refer to Resources, page 190, for this and other evaluation sources.

Reading and Writing Medium/a

The IEP team must also determine the student's reading and writing medium/a (please also see Reading and Writing, page 23). The 1997 Amendments to IDEA require the following:

> the IEP Team shall ... in the case of a child who is blind or visually impaired, provide for instruction in Braille and the use of Braille unless the IEP Team determines, after an evaluation of the child's reading and writing skills, needs, and appropriate reading and writing media (including an evaluation of the child's future needs for instruction in Braille or the use of Braille), that instruction in Braille or the use of Braille is not appropriate for the child. (Section 614(d)(3)(B)(iii))

This means that unless the results of evaluations in the areas listed—*including future need for braille*—rule it out, braille must be provided.

Over the past several decades and for a variety of reasons, braille was usually denied to students who had some vision or else the teaching of braille was delayed until the student was falling behind in school. The 1997 amendments to IDEA mandate that decisions about braille be based on an objective examination of the child's present and future need for the medium. This change in the law has the potential to make an enormous positive difference in the lives of blind/VI children. With the known correlation between competence in braille and both literacy and employment, there is no good reason to deny a student braille and every good reason to teach it.

APPROPRIATE PLACEMENT

In order for a blind/VI student to perform up to his or her capabilities in school, the child must be in the appropriate placement. As with keeping expectations appropriately high, it is useful to consider where the student would be placed if he or she were not blind/VI; that is likely to be the appropriate placement. If a blind/VI child is gifted, then that child should be in whatever classroom a gifted sighted child would be placed in. If the blind/VI child has moderate mental retardation, then he or she should be placed in the same setting a sighted child with moderate mental retardation would be in. Blindness/visual impairment should never be the deciding factor in placement.

Troubleshooting

Many blind/VI children end up in special classrooms or in reading or math groupings that are below their actual academic ability. Why does this occur? Consider these scenarios:

Jessica, a bright totally blind little girl, had had a successful year in a mainstream kindergarten. In May of that year, the principal of her elementary school sat down with the child's mother to discuss plans for first grade. "Of course we'll place Jessica in the low reading group," he said matter of factly. This surprised the mother, as the child's IQ had tested in the superior range and Jessica had been reading since mid-kindergarten.
"Why the low group?" she asked him. "She's already reading. Why not the middle group?"
"Because in the middle group, we expect them to understand what they read," he responded.

Michael, a braille reader who has some vision, has a fully sighted twin brother. Though Michael's academic abilities seemed higher than his brother's, Michael was placed in the school's Resource Room for reading and math, while his brother was placed in a regular classroom. Michael was never challenged academically in the Resource Room while his brother, who was eventually diagnosed with a learning disability, struggled in the mainstream class.

Why do placement mistakes like these occur? Unfortunately, placement decisions like these are based neither on an objective look at the student's abilities nor on the knowledge of how to make the education program of a blind/VI student work. They are instead based on negative assumptions, low expectations, and lack of information.

Blind/VI students are particularly vulnerable in assessment and placement situations, especially when it seems as if there is no *perfect* placement. It is very difficult for a blind/VI student to rise above low expectations on his or her own, because so much of what the student will be able to achieve, especially in the early grades, depends on the adults in his or her life making good placement decisions and providing appropriate, accessible materials. Don't let your staff's decisions be driven by the triple plague of fear of the unknown, ignorance of how things can/should be done, and the prejudice of negative assumptions about blindness/visual impairment. Make sure there is someone who has seen a blind/VI student flourishing in a regular classroom setting at least advising the IEP team.

Teaching Concepts on Schedule

To make it possible for the blind/VI student to progress at a pace appropriate to his/her cognitive ability and equal to that of sighted peers of similar ability, it is necessary for the student to learn concepts and skills on the same timetable as sighted students. It is surprisingly easy to delay the teaching of concepts and skills, even the teaching of braille, to blind/VI students. This can occur for a variety of reasons. For example, it may not be clear who has the responsibility to teach the concept or skill; someone may think the child needs more readiness skills; low expectations can play a role; perhaps no one has made adapted materials, or the adaptations are not working; or perhaps no one knows how a blind/VI person would perform the task. Whatever the reason, time can easily slip away and before you know it, the child has fallen behind.

This phenomenon tends to be noticed around third grade, when the material is becoming more complex and the pace is picking up. Naturally, it is harder to remedy the situation the longer it goes on. Work hard to prevent the problem by getting and keeping the student on grade level from the very beginning. Keep alert to signs that the student might be falling behind and look for ways to catch the problem before it burgeons—obtain or create extra practice materials for the student to do at home; find a qualified tutor; consider an extended school year.

ACCESSIBLE MATERIALS AND PRESENTATION OF INFORMATION

The blind/VI student will receive services directly from the TVI for a certain number of hours per week. But how will the student function in the classroom at all the other times, when the TVI is not present? The answer to this question is having accessible materials ready for the student. This is an absolute necessity for making the education of the blind/VI student work.

Having accessible materials ready means that the student will be able to fully participate in all classroom lessons and activities and will get the full benefit of your teaching throughout the day. The TVI teaches the student the specific skills he/she needs in order to take advantage of the classroom learning environment. The accessible materials allow the student to be taught and receive a full day's instruction along with everyone else. Accessible materials might be in the form of braille, large print, recorded information, verbal description, raised-line drawings, models, and so forth. For information on creating and obtaining accessible materials, please see Adapting Materials, page 147, and Resources, page 187.

Make sure you have the necessary materials on hand so that your blind/VI student can be included in math activities, map work, measuring, science experiments, and so forth. The blind/VI student needs training and practice in these areas just as sighted students do. The TVI can assist you with ideas and sources of materials.

Making the *presentation* of materials and information accessible is the other half of this essential equation. For example, it is possible to create an adaptation that looks very pleasing visually, but does not work tactilely. Or perhaps you are relying on verbal description to get the idea across, but the child needs something close-up or hands-on. Another common scenario is for the student to get only a very brief touch or quick glance at an object or mechanism, instead of getting a chance to examine it adequately. Or perhaps the concept is illustrated so inconsistently that the student cannot recognize it as the same.

If the student appears not to be getting a concept, check with the TVI and parents for suggestions on presentation. Please check Accessing the Curriculum: Classroom Techniques and Subject Guide, page 103, for specifics. Sometimes the solution will be as simple as putting something in the child's hands. The blind/VI child cannot be expected to learn without *looking*, any more than the sighted child can. Often what looks like a learning problem disappears when the child is provided with hands-on experiences.

Obtaining Accessible Textbooks

The TVI usually oversees the obtaining of accessible textbooks. Well in advance of the upcoming school year, classroom teachers must collect books and materials that will be used the following year and give them to the TVI to be sent out for enlarging or brailling. Get the books to the TVI as soon as possible (in some states this must be as early as February) so that books will be ready for the following September. The TVI or instructional materials center in the state or region then checks to see if the books have already been produced in alternative format or if they need to be produced from scratch. Several searchable databases exist for this purpose (see Resources, page 199) and information can also be obtained directly from the publishers. Regulations are being developed for new legislation which will make this process easier.

The blind/VI student will also need a regular print copy of every textbook. A print copy enables the blind/VI student to complete his/her assignments even if technology breaks down or cassette tapes get snagged. The large print user might use a regular print book when words are cut off in the enlarged copy or when the original color is needed to complete the assignment, for example, in mapwork, or for assignments requiring measuring. A regular print copy of textbooks enables the parents of both the large print and braille using student to be involved, see what is being taught, and support the child's education.

SERVICES FROM A TEACHER OF THE VISUALLY IMPAIRED AND OTHER SPECIALISTS

The TVI plays a pivotal role in making the education of a blind/VI student work. Following are the main responsibilities of the teacher of the visually impaired:

- Works directly with the blind/VI student. At various points in the student's progress, the TVI might instruct the student in concept development, self-help skills, and academic skills such as braille, using low vision aids, and using specialized materials. Instruction may take place before or after school, within the classroom, or in pullout sessions.
- Consults with classroom teachers regarding ways to include the blind/VI student, useful materials, resources, and so forth.
- Provides information on eye condition; makes recommendations for lighting, seating, helpful equipment, and so forth.
- Suggests strategies and sources of information regarding development and communication for children with additional disabilities.
- Conducts and/or assists with assessments; suggests appropriate modifications for tests and evaluations.
- Provides input at IEP meetings regarding progress and goals for blindness/visual impairment skill areas.

- Collects print textbooks and other school materials that will be needed the following school year in braille, large print, or recorded form.
- Brailles some materials for the classroom; adapts some materials into tactile form.
- Provides or recommends specialized equipment and materials.
- For braille readers in the early grades, writes in the print on student-produced braille papers so that the classroom teacher can read and correct the student's work.
- Provides in-service training to school staff.
- Makes referrals for other specialists, such as an O&M instructor, adaptive technology expert, and activities of daily living instructor.

How Much Service Is Enough?

Simply put, the student needs enough service from the TVI and other blindness/visual impairment specialists to ensure the development of the skills that will enable the student to participate fully in his/her educational program. The student and school district need enough service to ensure that the responsibilities listed above can be fulfilled.

The role of the TVI is especially important in the early years, when the child is developing the understanding of basic concepts, learning self-help skills, getting used to school, and learning to read and write. Beginning braille readers and newly blinded students usually require the highest levels of service from the TVI, but children who are delayed or in need of remediation also need high levels of service.

In order to develop literacy skills and fluent reading ability, young braille learners need braille lessons four to five times a week. In addition to the time they spend directly with the braille instructor, these students need materials ready in braille in all subjects. That way, as they take part in all class lessons and activities, they will be exposed to braille all day long, just as print readers are exposed to print.

Scheduling the student's time with the TVI can be challenging. Time is tight in a half-day kindergarten, for example, and the student will be very unhappy if he/she has to miss beloved subjects in first and second grades. Working to ease this situation is worth the effort. Use some creativity. Can lessons be scheduled for the morning right before school starts or for right after school? Perhaps this can be done for at least one or two of the lessons each week. Can the TVI integrate the lesson so that he/she can work with the child within the classroom?

The student's evaluations, current levels of performance, and IEP goals should identify areas of need. But in order for the education of a blind/VI student to work in the regular school, classroom teachers must be alert to any additional areas in which the student does not have age- or grade-level academic or self-help skills, or is beginning to fall behind. In order to meet the student's needs in these areas and keep him/her on grade level, a plan must be put in place. The plan might include more time with the TVI; it will often be a team effort, with classroom teachers, the TVI, and the parents all playing a role.

As the years go on and the student progresses in skills and independence, the TVI does less direct teaching. He/she begins to train the student in locating resources, ordering his/her own materials, and making his/her own arrangements with teachers for testing accommodations and the like. The TVI continues to play an important role, however, and will still be needed throughout the school years to handle the many other functions listed above.

TRAINING FOR CLASSROOM TEACHERS

It is very helpful if classroom teachers and aides receive some good hands-on training in how to work with a blind/VI student, how to include the student in class activities, how to adapt and present materials and concepts, and how to assist on the road to independence. If the TVI is unable to provide this training, school staff can try contacting the agency or commission that serves blind/VI people in the state; schools for the blind might offer outreach services; state chapters of consumer organizations such as the National Federation of the Blind and National Organization of Parents of Blind Children might be able to assist. You can also contact the author (please refer to About the Author, page 217.)

COMMUNICATE, COLLABORATE, APPRECIATE

The successful education of a blind/VI student in the regular school is definitely a team effort! Your student will make the most progress if there is an atmosphere of open, easy communication, collaboration, and partnership among all parties involved—classroom teacher, parent, student, aide or technical assistant, TVI, IEP team, and administrators. Open, easy communication enables everyone involved to understand expectations, goals, and plans and to tap into each other's creative ideas. It engenders an atmosphere of mutual respect and appreciation for the contribution each team member is making, an atmosphere in which the student can thrive.

SCHOOL ADMINISTRATORS CAN *MAKE IT WORK*

School administrators can have an enormous impact on how smoothly the education of the blind/VI child goes. Administrators can set a tone of welcome and acceptance, making it clear to all that the blind/VI student belongs at the school and encouraging staff to *make it work*.

Administrators can facilitate active partnership and teamwork among teachers, the TVI, parents, and any others involved, and set the tone for mutually respectful, open communication. Since blindness/visual impairment in children is a low incidence disability, chances are this is the first blind/VI child the school is educating, at least in anyone's memory. Administrators can make it safe for teachers and other staff to say the words "I don't know." Administrators can also set a tone of openness to information coming from outside sources, such as parents or organizations of blind adults and parents of blind children who have information about blindness/visual impairment to share.

Administrators can set an example of treating the student as a normal person. They can give staff permission to step back and not overprotect, thereby enabling the student to take the normal and necessary steps toward independence. (Please see School Administrators Must Be on Board, page 142.)

Choosing Teachers

School principals, who influence the educational path of all children, can make a positive difference for children with disabilities when they decide on teachers. The team may have developed the ideal IEP document and instructional guide; but the best IEP can be reduced to nothing if the teacher doesn't want the child in the room. It is not always possible to choose among teachers the one that would be best for the blind/VI student, but when it is possible, it makes sense to do it. Following are some characteristics to consider:

- Well-organized: A well-organized teacher will be able to plan enough in advance to get materials produced in accessible form.
- Calm, easy-going, flexible: It is easy to make mountains out of molehills in the education of a blind/VI child. A teacher who can

deal with the inevitable obstacles and delays that will crop up over the course of the school year will remain positive and upbeat.

- Confident: The teacher who deals well with students' differences will enjoy the year and will be more likely to achieve a positive outcome.
- Creative: Teachers who are creative in getting visual concepts across to blind/VI students will do a better job at building the student's foundation of knowledge.
- Good communicator: The classroom teacher of the blind/VI student, especially the young student, will need to communicate with, among others, the TVI and other blindness specialists, IEP team members, parents, and perhaps a classroom aide.
- Team player: A teacher who is able to plan, coordinate, collaborate with, and learn from others, and who would feel comfortable with new information, possibly from outside sources, will do best.

Of course blind/VI students, like all students, must learn to deal with the various personality types and teaching styles that children encounter as they move through their school years. But when school administrators can choose teachers with individual students in mind, the chances for a successful and smooth school year are heightened.

A high school principal who felt the 4 years a blind student spent in his school were very successful makes these suggestions for administrators (R. B. Padian, personal communication, March 25, 2004):

- Match the personality of the student with the personality of the teacher; they should be able to understand each other.
- Choose teachers who are problem solvers and who will go the extra mile.
- Match the student with teachers who are flexible and understand that learning can be measured in ways other than traditional paper and pencil.
- Capitalize on staff willing to take risks and try something new.
- Choose staff members who can look at students as individuals.
- Work with teachers to make sure the IEP is realized.
- Work with writers of the IEP to make sure it is specific about assessment; find ways to assess students that enable them to show what they know and have learned.
- Make changes in scheduling; make changes in classrooms; make it happen; make it work.

Hiring a Classroom Aide

Right from the interview process, the emphasis must be on an independent future for the blind/VI student. If it is determined that an aide is needed, look for an aide who can envision an independent future for the student, someone who is aware that blind/VI adults can and do live full and independent lives. Eliminate applicants who seek the job because they feel sorry for blind/VI children or want to help the handicapped. There is simply no room for indulgence or pity here.

Make it clear that the focus needs to be on the child and the child's progress, not on the aide and how much the aide is helping. The aide must be comfortable with the idea that his/her goal is to stop providing direct assistance and move into the background as soon as possible. During the interview process, the aide should understand that the aim is for him/her to set the stage for success for the student, and not to serve as a constant helper to a helpless person.

Please refer to The Role of the Teacher's Aide, page 123, for further discussion of these issues and for specifics on the responsibilities of an aide in a classroom with a blind/VI student.

Substitute Teachers and Teacher's Aides

In the early years it is very helpful to designate one or two substitute teachers and teacher's aides for the blind/VI student's classroom, and then to provide those individuals with some training on working with the blind/VI student. A little advance planning in this area can ensure that the substitute teacher/teacher's aide feels prepared for the day and that the blind/VI student will receive a full day's instruction, along with sighted classmates.

Building Preparation

A few simple adaptations can make it possible for your blind/VI student to be independent in the school building.

Label Classrooms

If classroom room numbers are high up above the doors, your student may not be able to see them. Likewise, if the school is an older building, it may not contain braille signage. You can easily add large print or braille room numbers to classroom doors.

- Cut large squares (about 4 × 4) from self-stick plastic sheets. Write in the room numbers in permanent marker and braille.

- Place the labels at about the child's eye or hand level on the door-knob side of the doorframe or wall. (That way the student can locate the room number whether the door is open or closed.)
- If rooms are referred to by teacher's name, subject, grade name, and so forth, add that to the label. For example, the label might read, "Room 3, Ms. Jones" or "Room 6, Math" in large print or braille.
- Label other doorways such as the cafeteria, library, office, boys' rooms, girls' rooms, maintenance closets, stairwells, and so on. If stairways are referred to by names, such as "the east stairs" or "the front stairs," add those words, too.

Floor Plan

- Provide your student with a bold-line or tactile floor plan. (Please see page 156 for a way to make a tactile floor plan.)
- The student who will be changing classes needs to become familiar with the layout of the building. This is especially important in the first year in a new building.

Schedule

- If your student will be changing classes, make his/her schedule available early so that he/she can practice getting from room to room.
- The student can also practice getting to and from the locker, getting to the restrooms from various classrooms, and getting to the library, office, and cafeteria.
- It will benefit the student to practice during the summer, before school starts.

Lockers

- An end locker, both in the hallway and in the gym locker room, will give the student more room to maneuver.
- The student might need two adjacent lockers due to oversize books.
- Substitute a key lock or a push button lock for a combination lock.
- Label the locker with a braille or large print number.

Book and Materials Storage

- You will need storage space for braille and large print books and other materials that begin arriving over the summer. A central location will make it easier to keep track of materials.

- Before the school year begins, transport books for each subject into the classroom(s).
- Make sure classroom book storage areas are accessible to the student.

PLAN A TIMELINE FOR INDEPENDENCE

It is up to the adults in the student's life to make the shift to independence actually happen. It is very simple to say "oh yes, we expect this student to be independent," but if no plan is put into place to ensure this result, it may never happen. It is very easy to put off actually doing the things that will ensure independence, because it often means doing things in a different manner, change, planning, perhaps taking what might feel like risks.

If independent functioning is the final destination, think hard about whether or not you've got your student on the road that leads there. Work backwards. Look down that road—what do you expect your student to be doing independently in 2 years—in 5 years—in high school—as an adult? Plan independence goals and strategies so that progress is made each year.

An independence plan must include goals for each year—or better yet, each semester or marking period. The independence plan will require reevaluation at close intervals so that the child's progress is constantly encouraged. Please refer to An Independence Plan, page 143 for a sample independence plan.

The student should become more and more independent as time passes. Think of it this way—the job should be done by the time the child leaves high school. How many years have you got left? After high school we want our students to go to the next step—a job, vocational school, college, a place of their own. If by age 18 a blind/VI student cannot take care of him/herself, travel independently, make his/her own arrangements for readers or transportation or whatever else he/she might use, then that student is not going to make it in the real world. So somewhere between the assistance we might give the preschooler and the independence we expect of a senior in high school, the shift must occur. Build it in; have a timeline; plan for a future of independence.

CHAPTER 6

WRITING IEP GOALS
AND OBJECTIVES

School personnel and families often have questions on how to create an appropriate individualized education plan (IEP) for a blind/visually impaired student. The process itself is the same for the blind/VI student as it is for any other student with an IEP. Observations and evaluations identify current levels of functioning, strengths, and needs; from the needs come the goals and objectives; and from the goals and objectives come the program and placement. Academic or developmental plans can then be made for the blind/VI student, just as they are for their sighted counterparts.

Blindness/visual impairment should never be the criterion for whether or not a student will be expected to learn a certain subject or master a certain skill. For example, blind/VI students take classes in algebra, geometry, biology, chemistry, physics, art, film, driver's education, and any number of subjects that might at first glance seem impossible or even of no use to a blind/VI person. Remember that blind/VI students need and deserve the same information and education as their sighted classmates.

Set goals according to the student's cognitive ability and developmental profile, not according to his/her level of eyesight. This means that the blind/VI student with high level cognitive ability will have the same academic expectations as sighted students with a similar cognitive level. For the blind/VI student who also has mental retardation, the goals will be the same as for sighted students with a similar developmental profile.

Making It Work: Educating the Blind/VI Student in the Regular School, 65–76
Copyright © 2005 by Information Age Publishing
All rights of reproduction in any form reserved.

The Process

Your student might fall into any of the following categories:

- Blind/VI and needing only adaptations in materials and presentation.
- Blind/VI with delays or additional disabilities that require some modification to curriculum or content.
- Blind/VI with significant additional disabilities that require a functional or developmental plan.

Whatever category your student falls into, the process will be the same. Assuming that the student has had a fair and appropriate evaluation (please see Setting the Stage for Success, page 51), the following are the steps to take:

- Think about what you would plan for this student if he or she were not blind/VI. Set academic or developmental goals just as you would for a sighted student with a similar learning profile.
  - If the blind/VI student has a learning or other disability that affects education, make the appropriate modifications to content, study guides, testing, etc., again, just as you would if this student were sighted.
  - If the student has no disabilities other than blindness/visual impairment, modifications in the academic goals will not be necessary, since that student would be expected to master the standard material.
- Add in the adaptations for blindness/visual impairment—such as specialized materials, hands-on or close-up presentation, and verbal description—wherever needed.

THE INSTRUCTIONAL GUIDE

If the academic or developmental goals for a blind/VI student are the same as those for a sighted student of similar cognitive ability, what is different in an IEP for a blind/VI student? One difference is the inclusion of an instructional guide for each goal, a how-to section which lists the materials and equipment that the student will need, since specialized materials are often the main adaptation needed for blindness/visual impairment (for example, braille instead of print). The instructional guide also lists strategies that will be effective with the blind/VI student to aid teachers in the presentation of materials and concepts.

An instructional guide might include such items as braille or large print books, raised-line or heavy-line graph paper, tactile or large print globes and maps, a computer adapted with screen enlargement or speech, and any other materials that would be of use for the student. (Please see Resources, page 187, for sources of educational materials.) The instructional guide would also specify who will be responsible for obtaining or creating the adapted materials.

The instructional guide should also contain strategies for the presentation of concept and materials, for example, "Verbalize what is written on the board or overheads," or "Place items in student's hands for examination," or "Provide desk copy in braille/large print of information presented on slides." Please refer to Specifics for Classroom Teachers, page 77, and Accessing the Curriculum: Classroom Techniques and Subject Guide, page 103, for strategy ideas.

Who creates the instructional guide? The TVI and other blindness/visual impairment specialists who work with or who have evaluated the child, teachers and teacher's aides (including those who taught or worked with the student in the previous year), parents, and other team members can all contribute their ideas and the benefit of their experience.

GOALS AND OBJECTIVES FOR THE SKILLS OF BLINDNESS/VISUAL IMPAIRMENT

The second difference in the IEP for a blind/VI student is the inclusion of goals and objectives related to the special blindness/visual impairment skills the student will be learning. For example, the student might be learning braille, cane travel, or how to use optical aids or adaptive technology. The various specialists involved with the student—TVI, O&M instructor, adaptive technology instructor, and perhaps others—are the ones who would write these goals and teach these skills. Classroom teachers might be asked to provide input for the formulation of goals. For example, the TVI might want to use vocabulary and concepts from classroom reading period as part of the student's braille instruction; the O&M instructor might want to use a route that the class travels every day for the practice of independent travel skills; the technology specialist might want the student to practice with class computer assignments.

Classroom teachers can have a positive influence on the student's progress in specialized skills in other ways, too. Teachers can speak with respect about the student's special skills and tools and encourage their use. In addition, teachers can keep in mind that the student needs sufficient time to practice and master these skills, and can provide practice time whenever possible.

If there is an aide in the classroom, he/she might be asked to come along on the student's lessons with specialists in order to learn about blindness/visual impairment skills and provide follow up and valuable practice opportunities for the student between lessons.

THE GOAL OF INDEPENDENCE

For most young blind/VI students, there will also be a third IEP difference—the inclusion of a goal of independence in the classroom. This goal needs to be explicitly stated in order to make sure the student is making continuous progress toward independence and to guard against overprotection, lowered expectations, and learned dependence—people doing things for the blind/VI student that the student could and should be doing for him/herself. This goal is important for students who are on grade level academically and for students with severe additional disabilities as well. The independence goal on each year's IEP should be a part of a timeline for independence (please see Plan a Timeline for Independence, page 64). Progress must be made each year.

For the youngest students, those in kindergarten and first grade, time for exploration must be included in the plan for independence. Through opportunities for guided discovery in the classroom, the cafeteria, the office, the gym, the library, the restrooms, and so forth, the student will not only learn the different areas of the school and build a good information base for the future, but will also learn how to find out this sort of information for him/herself.

One way to formulate objectives for the goal of independence is to think about your student's day in detail. Make a chart (Table 6.1) and see which tasks your student is able to perform independently; then you will be able to identify the next logical areas to work on.

Pinpoint three or four areas in which your student is not yet independent to work on first. When those goals are accomplished or are well underway, choose the next three or four. In this way you will not be leaving independence up to chance or good intentions. Remember, whether or not a blind/VI child is independent in school depends a great deal on the attitudes, expectations, and actions of the adults around him/her. If everyone involved is thinking about a timetable for independence, then it will happen.

An instructional guide will be of use for this goal, too, to help teachers lay the groundwork for independence in the classroom and facilitate independence in their blind/VI student in all areas.

Table 6.1.   Johnny Through the Day

Arrival

Gets off bus
Locates school entrance
Walks to classroom
Hangs up coat
Unpacks books
Places homework in homework bin
Finds seat

Lunchtime

Buys lunch
Carries tray
Finds seat
Opens containers
Eats lunch
Cleans up
Finds garbage can

School Day

Attends to lessons
Locates books
Finds pages
Does seatwork
Does groupwork
Changes classes
Goes to restroom
Walks in line

End of Day

Writes down assignments
Locates books and papers needed
Packs backpack
Gets in line
Walks to school exit
Finds bus line
Boards bus
Seats self on bus

Recess

Gets to playground
Finds playmates
Finds playground equipment
Walks in line back into building

CREATING A USABLE IEP IN ACADEMIC AREAS

A simple way to create a usable IEP for a blind/VI student is to start with the curriculum goals for each subject and a list of activities the teacher knows he/she will use. (If the student has additional disabilities that affect education, make the necessary modifications to content, etc.) Then go through the curriculum goals and teacher activities with the TVI and parents and jot down any adaptations, special tools, or materials that will be needed for blindness/visual impairment.

As you go through the list, you will find that some activities will need no adaptation at all, for example, an oral exercise on recognizing rhyming words. Others will require adaptation in materials and/or presentation. Some differences will be very minor, for example, when the class practices upper and lower case letters, the sighted children will use paper and pencil and the blind student will use the braillewriter and braille paper.

Other activities will require more extensive preparation. For example, if one of the activities is for students to create a fraction kit out of construction paper, the adaptation for the blind/VI student might be the following:

- Make a fraction kit for the student in advance out of lightweight cardboard.
- Provide a tactile fraction set (commercially available; can modify with braille) for the student to examine when the sighted students are looking at pictures of fractions and making their kits.
- Provide the cardboard set for the student to work with over a sheet of nonslip Dycem (see Resources, page 192) placed on the desk.

The TVI and often the parents will have other useful ideas for adapting materials and activities.

IF THERE IS AN AIDE

If there is an aide in the classroom, there should be a page in the IEP delineating his/her responsibilities. One of the most typical and most important responsibilities an aide might have is to create many of the adapted materials the student will use (see Adapting Materials, page 147). Other responsibilities of the aide in the areas of behind-the-scenes work, direct assistance, facilitating, and enrichment should also be written onto the sheet (see The Role of the Teacher's Aide, page 123). It is important to keep in mind that although the aide will assist the child, most of the aide's tasks, including direct assistance, should be aimed at facilitating independence and teaching the student to do tasks for him/herself, not simply doing things *for* the child.

As early as possible, work toward teaching the student to pay attention to and respond to the teacher and moving the aide into the background. In order for the child to progress in independence, the aide must be allowed, whenever the student is handling a task independently, to step back and do nothing without fear of criticism. Make sure that this, too, is written into the IEP, along with plans for phasing out direct assistance by the aide. Without a plan, it might never happen!

SAMPLE IEP GOALS AND INSTRUCTIONAL GUIDES

Following are sample IEP goals for a blind/VI second-grader who is learning both print and braille and who is on grade level. For a blind/VI student with a learning or other disability that affects education, make the necessary modifications to the academic goal, then add the blindness/visual impairment specifics as below.

For a student learning both print and braille, the IEP team would also decide when and under what circumstances the student would use each medium. That information would also be included in the IEP.

Sample Academic Goal

Goal 1: Johnny (a print and braille user) will complete the second grade curriculum in all academic subjects.

Instructional Guide

1. Materials in braille, large print, tactile, and other alternative media, including books, maps, measuring devices, clock, watch, calculator, etc., either created or purchased and ready for use.
2. Use of braille embosser to create braille worksheets, last-minute items, etc.
3. Use of computer and photocopier to enlarge materials.
4. Provide hands-on and close-up experiences whenever possible.
5. Use of manipulatives such as geometric forms, texture-enhanced math cubes, real money, etc.
6. Use of magnifier, felt-tip markers, book stand, colored acetate sheets, preferential seating and lighting, etc. as needed.
7. Use of Dycem, rubber mats, magnet and magnet board, push pins and corkboard, Wikki Stix, etc.
8. Send work home for preview when appropriate.
9. Send unfinished work home to be completed.
10. Share lesson plans in advance with TVI.
11. Consultation time with TVI, classroom teacher, and aide to review plans, share information and concerns, plan adaptations.
12. TVI introduces new braille contractions, signs, and formats in advance.
13. Lessons in using adaptive devices and techniques.
14. Classroom teacher awareness of braille and other alternative skills and devices student is learning and using.
15. Flexible standardized testing—tests in large print and/or braille; use of models, talking calculator, tactile ruler, extra time; use of reader.
16. Continuous reevaluation of student's organizational set-up so that Johnny can progress in independence.
17. Collect textbooks, workbooks, and other materials by April from next year's teachers to be sent out for brailling and/or enlarging.
18. Set of regular print textbooks for the home.
19. Maintenance of computer, braille embosser, and software as needed.

Sample Independence Goal

Goal 2:   Johnny will continue to progress toward independence in the classroom.

(Add objectives specific to your student.)

Instructional Guide

1.   Allow Johnny exploration time in the classroom.
2.   Allow practice time for skills.
3.   Provide discreet guidance as to classroom expectations Johnny has not yet mastered.
4.   Have all adapted materials ready for use.
5.   When necessary, quietly explain when routine instructions given to the class will be different for Johnny, reinforcing his growing understanding of such instructions.
6.   When necessary, remind Johnny to pay attention to the teacher and respond immediately to instructions.
7.   Encourage Johnny to work quickly.
8.   Aide to step back whenever Johnny is responding and working independently.
9.   Organize materials so that Johnny can easily locate and use them.
10.   Frequently reevaluate desk/organization systems to keep up with and encourage progress in independence.
11.   Aide to attend O&M lessons and provide follow-up between lessons.
12.   Encourage independent movement within the classroom and outside—to fountain, restroom, library, school office, playground, etc.

Sample Classroom Participation Goal

Goal 3:   Johnny will continue to develop classroom participation skills.

(Add objectives specific to your student.)

Instructional Guide

1.   Verbal guidance and explanations regarding the dynamics and expectations of participation in group activities.

2. Verbal description or physical modeling of movements and positions that may not be apparent without full visual information (e.g., raising hand and waiting to be called on).

3. Reminders, verbal prompting, use of signals (shoulder tap, snap, etc.) to keep Johnny focused and to encourage appropriate postures and participation.

4. Include Johnny in discussion even if he does not raise his hand.

5. Teach Johnny where attention should be focused when it may not be apparent without full visual information.

6. Describe routine movements and activities that may not be apparent without full visual information.

The above guides are meant only as samples of the possible strategies, adaptations, and tools teachers and student might use; your student may very well require a different set of strategies and adaptations. Check with the TVI and other blindness/visual impairment specialists, the student, and the family to find out the appropriate devices and techniques to use.

THE WORK BACKWARDS APPROACH

Use the work backwards approach as you formulate IEP goals and think about your student's future.

- Think about where you expect the student to be X years down the road.
- Think about where he/she is now.
- Determine how many years you have to work with.
- Determine what needs to happen in those years in order to get the student to the goal—what skills and tools does the student need to learn, who will teach them, how often will lessons be?
- Plan goals and objectives for each year.

For example, Paula is a fifth grader who uses both print and braille. She began braille training in third grade and is almost finished with learning the braille code. The delay in starting braille caused her math education to suffer. She reads and writes fairly well but is 2 years behind in math skills. Paula is very bright and everyone expects her to go to college.

What would working backwards look like for Paula? She is in fifth grade. The goal is college. In order to go to college she needs to take algebra, geometry, and a world language in high school. In order to take algebra, geometry, and a world language in high school she needs to be on grade level in math and reading/writing skills by eighth grade. In order to be on grade level by eighth grade she needs intensified math and reading/braille instruction during fifth, sixth, and seventh. Math and reading/braille goals for those 3 years can now be planned so that Paula's skills will be on grade level by eighth grade.

THE CHILD WITH SEVERE ADDITIONAL DISABILITIES

The process presented in this chapter is applicable for the student with severe additional disabilities, as well. In order to decide what will be taught, think about what the logical next step for the child would be if he or she were not blind/VI. Then add the adaptations, tools, and equipment for blindness/visual impairment. This student would need all the programming appropriate to a sighted child of similar cognitive and physical ability, along with the specialized expertise of a TVI who would assist with materials and ways of presenting items and concepts. Please see The Child with Additional Disabilities: Some Considerations, page 96, and Resources, page 203, for further discussion and ideas.

TRANSITIONING

The experience students gain at each level of schooling should launch them into success at the next level. This is true for all students, sighted or blind/VI. Think about your school's expectations and make sure your blind/VI student is exposed to all the necessary experiences and challenges that stimulate development and foster progress. If you notice areas in which the student is lagging, develop a plan of action with the TVI and parents to get the student caught up. The IEP can reflect this plan. Remember that blindness/visual impairment does not mean that the student must lag behind.

Meeting in Advance

Ideally, with the youngest students, the classroom teacher will have the opportunity to meet the student, the TVI, and the parents before school begins, perhaps over the summer or in the spring before he/she will have the student in class. It is likely that the teacher will have a lot of questions about how the whole process will work and an advance meeting can help to put his/her mind at rest.

Kindergarten

The blind/VI student should take part in all kindergarten activities. In kindergarten, it is typical to expect students to follow directions, pay attention in a group, finish a task, and work and play with other children. Fine and gross motor skills should be progressing, as should self-sufficiency in handling clothing, tying shoes, eating, toileting, and so forth. Be sure that your blind/VI student learns the letters, numbers, shapes, and colors, just as other children in the class do, and that problem-solving ability and concept development are moving along. Listening and speaking skills should be developing, as should literacy and math skills.

The blind/VI child will also be learning to orient and move about independently in the classroom. Encourage the student's autonomy and initiative. Discourage passivity. Pay extra attention to self-help skills, as adults tend to do things for the blind/VI student that the student should be doing for him/herself. Facilitate the student's interactions with others. Help the student learn to work up to speed.

Elementary School

The elementary school years are a time of great academic, emotional, and social growth. Students begin to take some responsibility for their own learning, remembering to write down assignments, bring home the correct books, and do their homework. They learn more about interacting with different personality types. By the end of elementary school, they are not babies any more.

Each year of elementary school should see the blind/VI student become more independent in mobility, study, self-help, and social skills so that he or she, like his/her sighted classmates, will be ready to handle the challenges of middle school. The balance must begin to shift from more protectiveness and monitoring of the student to more independence. The independence plan should be set up so that by the end of elementary school, the student is prepared for changing classes.

Middle School

In middle school it is time to give up vestiges of babyish treatment of the blind/VI student. The aide should be gone. The student should be learning to make decisions, handle materials, and discuss matters pertaining to blindness/visual impairment with teachers. The school-TVI-parent team will still play an active role in ensuring that any gaps in the student's independent functioning are addressed through training and opportunities to practice skills.

The student should be changing classes and participating in extracurricular activities. Take stock of the student's independence skills. This is the last chance to gain skills before high school!

High School

The blind/VI high school student should be taking classes commensurate with his/her interests and abilities, including college prep courses if the student is college bound. He/she should be included in all guidance department activities regarding college, technical school, or the world of work. (The student will be working with a vocational rehabilitation counselor, but he/she should still take part in all high school guidance activities.) The student should be well versed in the tools and techniques of blindness/visual impairment and should be independent in mobility.

Teachers should stay in contact with the TVI and the home to ensure that all skill areas are being addressed.

CHAPTER 7

SPECIFICS FOR CLASSROOM TEACHERS

If you are a classroom teacher reading this book, chances are you've never had a blind/visually impaired student in class before. Because blindness/ visual impairment in children is rare, most of the time it is a new experience for educators when such a student enters the school system. Take heart, however. The successful integration of blind/VI students into regular classrooms has been going on for many decades and long precedes the IDEA. You just need to learn how to do it. Teaching a blind/VI student can be an exciting career challenge with interesting information to learn, new strategies to employ, and different teaching techniques to try out that will enrich the learning experience of all your students.

Keep in mind the goals of independent, full participation in class and independent, full participation in life as you begin to work with your blind/VI student. Here are some of the things teachers can do to achieve these goals.

GUIDELINES FOR SUCCESS

This chapter will provide both the principles that underlie the successful education of a blind/VI student and the practical tips that can make it happen.

Making It Work: Educating the Blind/VI Student in the Regular School, 77–101
Copyright © 2005 by Information Age Publishing
All rights of reproduction in any form reserved.

Provide the Same Information, Experience, and Education

The classroom teacher needs to provide *the same or at times equivalent* information, experience, and education for the blind/VI child as for the sighted children in the class. In order to function on an equal basis with sighted peers within the classroom and in order to prepare for the future as an independent adult, the blind/VI student needs the same education experience that sighted children receive. The blind/VI student needs the same foundation, the same knowledge base, the same set of understandings. Providing the same educational experience for the blind/VI student might entail no modifications at all to the lesson you are presenting. It will often entail providing materials that have been adapted into accessible form. Sometimes it will entail giving the student a close-up or hands-on peek at equipment or materials before an activity takes place. It will definitely entail making sure the blind/VI student is included in the lesson or activity in an equal way.

Troubleshooting

Sometimes a teacher cannot think of a way to include a blind/VI student in an activity or does not think the blind/VI child is capable of doing a certain task. To solve this dilemma, the teacher might decide to make the child a special helper. Perhaps all the other students are settling down to an academic task and the teacher says to the blind/VI student, "You sit next to me and help me pass out the crayons." When situations like this occur, the blind/VI child is not getting the equivalent educational experience. Occasionally this might be acceptable, but certainly not if it occurs frequently.

A way to figure out how to include the blind/VI student in an activity is to analyze what is to be learned and think about possible ways to get the message across. Usually a simple adaptation can be made. If you can't think of a way, ask someone else—the TVI, the parents, a blind/VI adult—for ideas. But don't leave the child out.

Assume Responsibility

The classroom teacher must assume the same responsibility for the education of the blind/VI child as for the education of the sighted children in the class. Be knowledgeable about the blind/VI student's academic progress. If you grade the papers of the other children in the room, grade the blind/VI student's papers, too. If you keep track of the reading, writing, and math skills of the other children, keep track of the blind/VI student's, too. Make sure your student is a true member of the class, not just a student who is assigned to your room but whose education is someone else's responsibility. A successful learning environment for the blind/VI student certainly relies on teamwork, but the classroom teacher is really the key figure.

Make sure *you* are the one doing the teaching! Don't let a separate classroom within a classroom develop in which you teach the class and an aide teaches the blind/VI student. Speak and interact directly with the blind/VI student as you would with any other child in the class. Don't let an aide or the TVI become an intermediary between you and your student.

Encourage the Use of Alternative Skills

The alternative skills of blindness/visual impairment enable the blind/VI student to participate independently and to complete tasks without frustration. If teachers understand and appreciate the effectiveness of these skills and encourage their use, the student will progress in them all the more. Please see The Skills and Tools of Blindness, page 23.

Teachers and other staff members need not become experts in blindness/visual impairment skills. All that is needed is to become familiar with the general sequence of the skills, offer appropriate support as the child is working toward mastery, and provide opportunities whenever possible for the child to practice.

A Sampling of Alternative Skills

- Information can be reliably perceived through the sense of touch. The blind/VI student will look at objects with his/her hands (or with hands along with eyesight) and will get information tactually just as sighted children get it visually.
- Braille reading and writing is the equivalent of print reading and writing. Braille can be used to convey everything from simple children's stories to music, languages, higher math, and chemistry.
- The blind/VI student will use O&M skills to move about more and more independently as time goes on. Make sure your student is allowed and encouraged to make age-appropriate progress toward independent mobility.
- The cane is an essential O&M tool which is key to the child's independence (see Cane Travel, page 39). Respect the cane and encourage its use.

- The child will also learn to use sound, memory, mental mapping, an awareness of slopes and textures beneath his/her feet and cane, and other O&M skills to move about independently.

- Give the student opportunities to explore the room hands-on or close up, so that he/she can find out where things are placed and make a mental map. (Perhaps the student can visit the classroom in the summer.)

- The student will develop and use the other senses, such as hearing, smell, and body position. "That sounds like the art closet door opening in the back of the room. Yup, time for art; I hear Mr. Mullin getting the cans of paint out."

- The student will develop and use memory. "Mrs. Alcott, I remember your saying that you would store the braille atlas in the supply cabinet. Would you get it out for me, please?" Or perhaps, "We can't have my reading conference on Thursday afternoon, Mr. Meyers; that's the day the computer specialist will be coming."

- The student will develop and use sound localization, the ability to tell where a sound is coming from. You will be able to make use of this skill to direct the student to and from locations. For example, you might say, "Here's a seat, right here," while tapping on the back of a chair. Or you might say, "Go over and join Sarah's group. Walk in the direction of her voice."

- Asking questions to gain information is another important skill the student will develop. The student might ask, "Who just walked into the room?" or "Is this the bus for the fourth grade skating party or the bus for the third grade trip to the zoo?" or "I'm on my way to Mr. Reynolds' room. Am I heading in the right direction?"

- The student will learn to determine when to ask for assistance. He/she will also learn how to give a polite but firm "No, thank you" when assistance is not needed.

Build in the Expectation for Independence

Build in the expectation, the instruction, and the practice time for independence skills. Once the expectation for independence in all areas is in place, then the critical issue becomes making sure the child is taught the skills he/she needs in order to actually function independently and is given plenty of opportunities to practice. As with learning any skill, practice time is essential in order for the student to make progress and attain mastery. When we teach long division or converting fractions to decimals, for example, we give the students plenty of problems to practice on. Likewise, when the child is learning the way to the office, we need to provide opportunities for him or her to go there. Without practice the skills won't develop.

Expect independence in all areas—academic, social, and personal. Can your blind/VI student sit and complete a worksheet with the same level of independence as the sighted students in the class? Are his/her social abilities moving along? How is the student doing with personal skills—eating lunch, managing in the bathroom, putting on his/her coat? If you find that your young blind/VI student is not as independent as the other students in academic, social, and self-help skills, then make sure that independence goals in these areas are included in the student's education plan. Make sure also that someone is teaching the child the skills. The adults in the student's life must set up the learning environment so that the student progresses in skills and does not continue in dependence.

If there is an aide in your classroom, make sure the aide's work area is not next to the blind/VI student's! The student's desk must be set up *for the student's independent functioning*. Make sure the aide is not hovering over the student. Please see The Role of the Teacher's Aide, page 123.

Be a Team Member, Be a Good Communicator, Be Flexible

Experienced classroom teachers who have had a blind/VI student in class emphasize the need for good communication and the sharing of ideas. The education of a blind/VI student is definitely a team effort. Chances are the team working with your student has never had a blind/VI student before, so no one should feel like a failure if something that seemed like such a great idea flops when actually tried with the student. If your idea didn't work, consult the TVI or give the parents a call to find out what works at home. Check with the student, too, for helpful feedback. When school, home, and TVI all work together, the student makes the most progress.

Teamwork and advance planning will make it possible to get the background work done—generating ideas, adapting materials, collecting special items—so that the blind/VI student can be included in all activities. Flexibility will enable teachers to handle the glitches that will inevitably occur—books that don't arrive on time, materials that don't work well, technology that breaks down—and come up with appropriate alternatives. Good communication helps everyone keep the goals in mind and will give your student the best chance at success.

Don't Act on Assumptions

Make it a point to learn about the ways successful, competent blind/VI adults accomplish tasks. Remember that blind/VI people do go to work, cross busy streets, navigate subway systems. Remember, too, that you are preparing your blind/VI student for an independent future and that the key is having the skills to do the job.

There will be situations in which you feel fairly certain that your student will not be able to do the task. Instead of acting on that assumption and either doing the task for the child or keeping him/her from doing it, give the child some instruction or guidance and let him/her give it a try. Don't necessarily rush to help. Allow time for independent problem solving. You might discover that your assumption was not true. If you find that the student really cannot do what is required, then the next step is to make sure someone teaches him/her how to do it. Depending on the task, this could be you, a classroom aide, the TVI or other specialist, or the parents.

Proceed carefully in areas where you assume the child will need help. Examine your beliefs about blindness/visual impairment as you work with your student throughout the year. Be open to changing and raising your expectations. Your beliefs and expectations will unquestionably affect the way you treat the student. Don't act on assumptions, question them!

PRACTICAL TIPS

After you work with a blind/VI student for even a little while, you will probably find that the simple adaptations that enable you to include the student become second nature to you. Many classroom teachers report that the increased emphasis on the other senses enriches the learning experience for all the children.

Not all of the tips and techniques in this section will be applicable to all students. Feel free to pick and choose the ones that make sense for your student's age, grade, and experience.

Blindness Awareness for the Class

A blindness awareness presentation is a good way to foster understanding, acceptance, and respect for the blind/VI student in the class. A blindness awareness presentation can help sighted students become familiar with the tools and techniques of blindness/visual impairment and learn ways to interact with and include the blind/VI student in activities. The session can help students realize that their blind/VI classmate is a student just like them who will be learning the same subjects and doing the same assignments but who might be using different tools to get the work done. A blindness awareness presentation can be made by the TVI, a skilled blind/VI adult, the student him/herself along with a parent, or a volunteer from an organization such as the National Organization of Parents of Blind Children (see Resources, page 208).

Beware of Simulation

Teachers are often tempted to use simulation exercises to raise awareness and to show students what it is like to be blind. In these exercises, sighted students don a blindfold and then attempt to perform various tasks or walk around the school building being guided by a classmate to build trust.

What are the goals of such exercises? Sighted students will probably have trouble performing tasks under blindfold that they are accustomed to doing with their eyesight. Is the goal to show them how hard it is to be blind? Sighted students will probably be nervous giving over their safety to a guide who is walking them around. Is the goal to show that blind people are helpless and dependent and must put their trust in good-hearted sighted people in order to get anywhere or to keep from falling down a flight of stairs?

Before you embark on such an activity, think about what you want the students to learn. Wearing a blindfold for a little while might show what it would be like to suddenly lose vision, but it certainly does not show what it is like to be blind. Real blind/VI people learn a series of skills that enable them to perform tasks without or with very little eyesight. Likewise, real blind/VI people learn mobility skills so that they can trust themselves and get where they need to go.

If children are blindfolded but are not taught any of the skills that real blind/VI people use, they are likely to emerge from a simulation experience feeling that blindness/visual impairment is scary, sad, and difficult. Is this what you want them to think blindness/visual impairment is like? Instead of fostering acceptance, understanding, and respect, these exercises engender sadness, fear, and pity. Instead of thinking of their blind/VI classmate as a potential friend, students can end up feeling more distant from their blind/VI classmate and feeling sorry for him or her.

A Better Way

A better way to foster understanding and promote friendships is through a presentation that will promote respect for the blind/VI student and the skills and tools he/she will be using.

Discussion Topics

The information in chapters 2, 3, and 4 of this book can serve as starting points for discussion. Your students might enjoy taking the quiz and completing the worksheets on pages 16, 31, and 32. Possible discussion topics include the following:

- How do blind/VI people accomplish tasks?
- What jobs do blind/VI people do?
- How might blind/VI people use their other senses?
- What skills and tools do blind/VI people learn in order to do their schoolwork, get to the supermarket, cook a meal, do their jobs?
- How does braille work?
- How can we get our blind/VI classmate into games?

Special Items

Ask your presenter to show students items such as print-braille and large print books, braille and large print rulers and tape measures, a braillewriter or slate and stylus, a talking and large print calculator, a talking dictionary, a coloring screen, braille and large print playing cards, a bell ball, and so forth.

Cane Travel Discussion and Demonstration

A cane travel discussion and demonstration is effective in helping students understand that their blind/VI classmate will be learning travel techniques that will enable him/her to move about safely and independently. Discussion topics can include the following:

- How do blind/VI people move about independently?
- How can a person get information without eyesight?
- How does the cane work?

In addition to demonstrating basic cane use, your presenter can show students how a blind/VI person gets information through the cane, identifies different surfaces, gets around obstacles, and goes up and down stairs.

Trying It Out

Give students some hands-on experiences with the tools and techniques of blindness/visual impairment. Here are some examples:

- Have the blind/VI student or adult presenter write each child's name in braille on a piece of paper that the children can take home.

- Point out that the number five on a phone pad usually has a tactile marking that blind/VI people use as a reference point when dialing; let students try to find the marking using their sense of touch. Some might then want to locate the other numbers.

- Children often wonder how a blind/VI person can eat without being able to see. Put several plastic forks and spoons in a bag; have the students reach in the bag and retrieve either the spoons or the forks. They will see how easily they were able to discern which was which. Then have them close their eyes and see if they can get a spoon to their mouths. Point out that they probably brush their teeth without looking.

- Brainstorm with the class about how people could accomplish various tasks without eyesight.

- Set up role play situations in which one child closes his/her eyes and a partner tries to show him/her an object. Students will soon see that using words and putting the object into the blind/VI child's hands will be effective.

- Brainstorm ways to get the blind/VI child into games. For example, in a game of kickball, instead of rolling the ball to the blind/VI student, the ball could be placed in front of him or her.

Activities like these teach skills and broaden awareness. The blind/VI child will probably enjoy the attention given to his/her methods; the sighted children will enjoy the success they experienced and the understanding they gained and will feel empowered to interact with their blind/VI classmate. These experiences will foster the idea that their blind/VI classmate can be a friend and an equal, and friendship and equality beat charity and pity any day.

Teach the Blind/VI Student the Workings of the Classroom

Blind/VI children in the early grades, like all children, need to learn about classroom routine. Your blind/VI student may need to learn procedures like the following:

- To focus on the teacher;
- To listen and pay attention when the teacher is talking even if his or her name is not specifically used;
- To respond quickly to instructions, for example, by getting out a book or getting ready to write;

- *How* to respond—for example, when to raise a hand, when to lower the hand, when to answer out loud, when to answer in unison, how to face the teacher so the teacher can tell that he/she is paying attention;

- How to interpret questions expressed in classroom language. For example, in ordinary English a who question would be answered with a name, but in the classroom, "Who can tell me what 5 plus 2 is?" means, "Raise your hand." A how many question would ordinarily get a number for an answer, but in the classroom, "How many of you put the big hand on the 3?" means raise your hand if you did it that way. Hearing the teacher say your name (getting called on) usually means, "Say the answer out loud."

- That sometimes the teacher will give instructions that do not pertain to a student using a braille or enlarged worksheet. For example, the teacher might say, "Now turn your paper over and look at the first picture on side two" or "Let's look at the sentence at the bottom of the page." It is very possible that the adapted sheet is not set up the same way. The young student may need clarification for a while, may need help in locating the section, and may need to do reality checks—"but not me, right?"

  Be patient with the student for whom this is difficult. After all, the young student just learned to pay attention to the teacher and now we're asking him/her to make determinations about when to ignore what the teacher said and figure out his/her own directions!

- When and where to move in the classroom;

- How to interpret the activity going on around him/her in the classroom and determine what others are doing;

- To work at an appropriate pace (please see the section on pace on page 93);

- Eventually, how to figure out all of the above by him/herself.

Be More Verbal

- Adding a bit of verbal description will help the blind/VI student interpret what is going on in the classroom. For example, "I see Table 1 has finished cleaning up and is sitting very quietly. Table 1, you may line up for recess." Knowing what is going on and eventually knowing what to expect, will help the student be a full participant.

- Use names when calling on children. This will enable the blind/VI student to learn who is in the class and where each child sits. It will also help the child begin connecting names to voices. Encourage students to use names, too. This information will enable the blind/VI student to better follow what is going on in the classroom and will encourage social interaction, as well.

- Use precise words in place of vague statements and/or motions. For example, when modeling an action, instead of saying "Fold the paper like this," say, "Fold the paper lengthwise." Instead of "It's over there," say, "It's to the left of my desk."

- When referring to objects, think about attributes in addition to color, such as shape, weight, texture, size, use, and location. Instead of "Sam, please put it in the red box," try "Sam, put it in the small plastic box at the left end of the bookshelf."

- Give the blind/VI student the opportunity to get things for you by describing the object as above and then giving directions to the location. For example, "Would you please get me my lunchbag? It's the small canvas bag on the back right corner of my desk." Or "Michael, please get the chalk boxes from the art closet. Go straight back to the wall and then look for the third door on the right. The shelf you want will be about nose high."

- Explain your routine a bit to help the blind/VI child interpret situations which he/she cannot see. "I'm so glad you're all being quiet as I get the snack ready." The student will soon be able to identify many activities by their sounds.

- Explain situations that are completely visual, especially those that cause the children to laugh or exclaim. For example, the school nurse comes to the door, puts a finger to her lips, points to a child, and silently beckons the child to her. Or the children burst out laughing because a student from another class pokes his head into the room and makes a funny face. Let the blind/VI student in on what is so funny.

- Verbalize what you write on the board or on overheads; spell out words and names when needed (see section on Boardwork, page 103).

- Add a few words of explanation when the illustrations in a storybook help carry the plot since the blind/VI student will probably not have access to the picture. "Ah, ha! What do we see Teddy Bear holding in the picture? Yes, he's holding the key that was lost!"

- Use normal language such as *look* and *see*. There is no need to avoid these words. The blind/VI child will soon learn that sighted people look with their eyes and blind/VI people look with their eyes and/or fingers.

the Blind/Visually Impaired Student's
ion

- ...... ways to adapt activities so that the blind/VI student can participate (not every activity will require adaptation). Don't ask *if* it can
  be done, ask *how* can we do it. Don't make the blind/VI student a
  special helper; he/she needs the same educational experiences
  other children get.
- Have all adapted materials ready in advance.
- Place braille or enlarged books in the bookshelf along with other
  classroom books for recreational reading.
- The partially sighted student will probably benefit from close-up
  seating. Also check with the TVI, the parents, and the older student
  him/herself to see if he/she is sensitive to glare, variations in lighting, and so forth.
- If you move around the room a lot as you teach, pass by the blind/
  VI student's desk to give a hands-on or close up look at objects.
- Model movements for songs, fingerplays, or exercises that you want
  the whole class to learn by moving the blind/VI student through the
  motions. Other students can learn by observing teacher and student while the blind/VI student learns by experiencing the movements. Let the parents know if the child is having trouble with a
  movement. Perhaps it can be practiced at home.
- Use sound localization to direct the child. For example, he/she can
  join the other children by moving toward their voices and can come
  when called by walking toward your voice. The blind/VI student can
  also listen for footsteps in order to follow in line and can locate a
  chair or other objects when you tap them with your hand.
- Hands-on or close-up opportunities along with verbal description
  will make experiences much more meaningful for a young blind/VI
  child. For example, on a trip to the nurse's office, let the child
  explore by touch or get a close-up look at the scale or other characteristic objects.
- For objects that ordinarily would not be handled, let the child tactually examine them before or after the activity, if possible.
- Tell the child to "look with two hands" or "use both hands" when
  examining something tactually; a touch with one hand or a few fingers gives almost no information.
- Position crayons correctly in the child's hand for normal muscle
  development. Use raised-line drawings and a coloring screen (see

page 155) for sensory feedback and to make coloring more
ing to the blind/VI student.

Facilitate Independence in Participation

The aim is always for the student to participate as independently as he
or she can at any given time. For the blind/VI student, the goal of independence must be kept constantly in mind because it is very easy to fall
into doing things for the child or putting off taking the time to teach the
child how to do a certain task. Please refer to The Role of the Teacher's
Aide, for a more in-depth discussion of independence in the classroom.

- Help from teachers and aides should be aimed at teaching the student to do the task for him/herself, not doing it for the student.
- Offer information instead of help. Instead of getting an object for
  the child, for example, give the child a chance to find it by describing its size, shape, and location. Then give the child enough time to
  explore and correct mistakes before you give more prompts.
- The student should be able to learn any task that is repeated each
  day, such as setting the tables for snack time or lining up for recess
  or dismissal. Assume that the child can learn the task.
- If the child is not doing something the other children are doing,
  teach him/her how. If something must be done for a student on a
  regular basis, let the parents know. Perhaps it can be worked on at
  home.
- Again, make sure the student's desk is set up for his/her independent functioning. If there is an aide in the classroom, make sure the
  aide's work area is well away from the student's.

Keeping Organized

- For the primary grade student, vertical snap-together bins from an
  office supply store can be placed on the student's desk to hold
  books and folders.
- Volumes of braille or large print books not in use at the moment
  can be kept in bookshelves or boxes in the classroom. The student
  should have easy access to the books so he/she can get the next volume when it is needed.
- For a braille user taking notes on paper (as opposed to using an
  electronic notetaker), oversized folders or binders can help keep

work organized. Because of the bulk of paper that can accumulate, the student might keep most of the papers at home, organized by subject. When it is time for you to check notebooks, the student can bring the work in. If print has not been written in, ask the student to read the notes to you.

- The student who takes notes on an electronic notetaker can print out the notes for you.

If the team has done its job, as the student gets older and gains more skills, he/she will not need a high level of assistance with all of these tasks. The student should be learning how to handle his/her own work and participate in class independently.

Facilitate Social Interaction

Making friends and having normal social interaction with peers is not always easy for the blind/VI child. Some children have had very little opportunity to socialize and so have little experience with making and keeping friends. Some children lack social skills. And some face the bias that is still present in our society against people who are different in some way.

Classroom teachers can aide in this challenge in several ways:

- Foster an atmosphere of friendliness, respect, empathy, and acceptance during all activities, during class time, during specials, at lunch, and at recess. Emphasize everybody's worth, everybody's value, everybody's contribution. A tone of acceptance and inclusion in the school will help all students feel good about themselves and encourage them to do their best.

- Use positive language when you speak about blindness/visual impairment and the tools and techniques the student is using. It will not help your blind/VI student if others think he/she is inferior or feel sorry for him or her.

- Try to equalize things among the students. Don't let the blind/VI student become a burden; don't let the other children feel the blind/VI student is always in need of help. Promote friendships, not only a helping relationship. Identify situations in which the blind/VI student can provide help to others.

- Make sure the student is seated with peers and not off to one side or corner of the room alone. He/she may need extra room for

equipment or need to be near an electrical outlet, but these needs
must be met without isolating the student from peers.

- Have all necessary materials prepared in advance so that the blind/
  VI student can fully participate in all activities.
- When conducting group activities, help the blind/VI student
  become part of a group and facilitate the child's participation, if he/
  she needs such assistance.
- If the student is not age appropriate in social behavior, do some
  coaching. Teach him/her how to respond when someone makes an
  overture to play. Tutor the other children as well. For example,
  "You know, if you want to play with Megan, you have to say her
  name, because she can't see you waving to her."
- Remind the child to face the person with whom he/she is speaking.
  Eye contact, whether actual or positional, is an important social
  skill to develop.
- Teach the child to face the correct way in general. A rule of thumb
  is to give the blind/VI child the same instruction or correction you
  would give a sighted child who was situated in an inappropriate
  way.
- If applicable, remind the child to keep his/her head up and to stand
  up straight. Often this is best accomplished by telling the whole
  class "let's all stand nice and tall" instead of bringing attention specifically to the blind/VI student.
- If applicable, remind the child not to press his/her eyes or engage
  in other socially inappropriate behaviors. Often putting an interesting object in the child's hands or giving the child something better
  to do can diminish this kind of behavior.

Behavior Issues

If your blind/VI student often exhibits poor behavior, it is important to
identify the root of the problem so that a solution can be found. Here are
some things to think about:

- Does your student have an additional disability that affects behavior, such as autism or ADD?
- Does your student lack communication skills and therefore must try
  to tell you things by acting out?
- Is the student bored? Is he or she sitting in class with nothing to
  look at (tactily or visually) and nothing to do?

- Is the expectation level too low? Is the student ready for the next level of challenge?
- Is the challenge level too high? Is the child feeling frustrated?
- Does the child understand what is expected of him/her?
- How is the social environment? Is the child experiencing rejection? If so, is the blind/VI student contributing to the problem?

School Work

For the most part the ideas in this section refer to younger students or to older students who have experienced delays. As your student gains more and more knowledge and skills for independent participation, encourage him or her to make decisions about which methods to use for various assignments. With the guidance and supervision of teachers and parents, the student can begin making these decisions as early as third grade.

The special items referred to in this section can all be found in Resources, page 187; also see The Role of the Teacher's Aide, page 123, and Adapting Materials, page 147, for more information on creating materials and independent participation for the blind/VI student.

- Help the student organize the workspace. Have a clear place in front of the child for working; help him/her decide on common sense places to put materials where they can be easily reached.

- When the student needs to read from a book or worksheet and write answers on a separate sheet, position the book or worksheet where the student can read comfortably. The print user might use a slanted reading stand. The braille user can have the book or worksheet on the desk next to the braillewriter or on a special shelf that fits over the braillewriter. (The answer sheet would be in the braillewriter.) Caution: If your student uses an over-the-braillewriter shelf, make sure the shelf is at an appropriate height; if it is too high, the child will have to read with arms raised—a very uncomfortable position.

- When manipulatives are used, place them in a small box or tray so they will not fall off the desk.

- For marking answers, the blind/VI student can use a crayon, marker, pencil, small pieces of Wikki Stix, magnets and magnet board, or push pins. For braille users, marking with crayon and pencil is usually faster than the other alternatives above, but does not enable the student to check his/her own work. With Wikki Stix, magnets, and push pins, the braille user can check his/her own work. With crayon, pencil, and Wikki Stix, answers can be saved and work can be displayed or taken home.

- When you ask the class to draw a picture of their favorite part of the book, the blind/VI student can create a word picture, either by dictating or writing about the part of the story he/she liked the best. For example, the student might say, "Kitty is up in the tree and the fire fighters come and put up their ladder to get her down."

- For learning to cut with scissors, your student can begin with just cutting across a sheet of paper. Using slightly firmer paper (about the weight of braille paper) can facilitate the process, as can taping one corner of the paper to the desk. Cutting fringe along the edge can come next. Some students would benefit from easy-grip scissors.

- For cutting along a line, make the line more visible with black marker or make it raised using puffy paint, Hi-Mark, Wikki Stix, a tracing wheel, or braille dots. Again, firmer paper will be easier for the student to handle.

- Many teachers make or have the students make large, tactually interesting print letters when teaching the letters and letter sounds. This would be fine for the blind/VI child who will be using print, but all that energy and enthusiasm needs to be spent on the *braille* letters for the braille learner! Ask the TVI for assistance with presentation ideas.

- The blind/VI student can keep a journal, make entries in a spelling or vocabulary log, write books for classroom publishing, and participate in all language arts activities. Folded and stapled pages or journal book pages can be rolled into the braillewriter. Regular braille paper or heavy-line paper can be bound in a decorative way to produce a book. Tactile or three-dimensional illustrations can be added. Be creative—many ideas will work!

- For information conveyed on posters, vocabulary logs, schedules, etc. displayed around the classroom and in the halls, make a copy for the student to keep in a binder or folder at his/her desk.

Pace

The blind/VI student may need extra time in the early grades in order to complete tasks independently. This must be balanced with general classroom expectations. There will be times when it is worth allowing the student the time to finish one job independently even if he/she must skip another job. At other times, it will be more important for the student to change activities along with the rest of the class. You'll have to use your judgment. The answer to the dilemma over the long run is to teach the student good techniques so that he/she can work faster.

If you find that your blind/VI student is consistently working more slowly than the others in the class, here are a few ideas for helping him/her learn to work at an appropriate pace. Sighted children use visual cues to figure out how fast they should be moving. They might look at the clock on the wall; they might glance at their classmates' desks to see who is still working on the first side of the page and who has gone on to side two. You can provide equivalent nonvisual cues for your blind/VI student. Point out the rustling sound of pages turning so he/she can listen for how fast classmates are going. If the child can tell time, a braille or talking watch or clock could help. Periodically give verbal cues such as "About half of our time is up. You should be on number four or five by now."

Here is another aspect of pace to consider. Classroom teachers are often told that the blind/VI student will take longer to accomplish school-work and therefore should be expected to do only part of the assignment. Teachers are often advised, for example, to have the student do only the even-numbered problems or every other row or only enough to demonstrate that the student understands the concept.

It is true, especially in the early grades, that blind/VI students might take longer to complete certain assignments. This tends to happen when the student is also in the process of mastering the blindness/visual impairment skill necessary to complete the assignment. For example, the student might be learning how to set up math problems on the braillewriter; or the child might be physically doing more—moving from a workbook page on the desk to an answer sheet in the braillewriter—while sighted classmates are simply writing in the answers on a workbook page.

Sometimes it might seem sensible to cut back a little on one part of the workload while the child is learning or mastering a new skill. If you do, make sure you also build in a plan to get the child working up to speed as soon as possible. When blind/VI children become adults and go out on job interviews they won't get the job if they have to say "I can only do half the work" or "I can only do the even-numbered problems!" Again, we must keep in mind that in addition to teaching our children math and reading and history, we are also preparing them to be adults.

Another situation that might cause a student to work at a slow pace is an inadequate reading medium. Partially sighted students often cannot keep up with class reading because it is a struggle or too fatiguing to read a lot of print. If your student requires significant magnification for all print work, then that student probably needs braille in addition to print. This is also true if your student cannot read back his/her own notes. For more information on reading media, please see The Skills and Tools of Blindness, page 94.

Have Accessible Materials Ready

In order for your student to participate in your class fully and indepen-dently, accessible materials must be ready for his/her use (please see The Role of the Teacher's Aide, page 123, and Adapting Materials, page 147). The student who is learning braille will spend a certain number of hours each week receiving instruction from the TVI; the rest of the time he/she will be receiving instruction from you. With accessible materials, the blind/VI student will have the same opportunities to develop literacy and academic skills that the sighted children have. With accessible materials, you can ensure that throughout the school day the student will be included in all activities and will receive the full benefit of all lessons.

Troubleshooting

If you feel that your blind/VI student just isn't catching on to a lesson or concept, *make sure you put something into the child's hands!* Many times the problem is not with the student and his/her ability to learn, but with the presentation of the information.

A tricky aspect of this is that sometimes adaptations that seem like a good idea or look good visually, simply do not work in the hands of the student. If this occurs, keep trying different materials until you find the ones that work with your student. Consult with the TVI and the parents for ideas on what might work. Again, don't assume that the problem lies with the child.

Teacher Tools

Many special materials are available to aid in the education of blind/VI students. Sources for the special items listed in this section can be found in Resources, page 187.

- To make quick braille labels, use a braille labeler and self-stick labeling tape (Dymotape).
- To make instant raised-line drawings, the Sewell Kit, a coloring screen, or Wikki Stix can be used.
- Hi-Mark, T-shirt markers, and Elmer's glue can also be used to make raised-line drawings, but they must be used in advance to allow for drying time.
- Self-stick Velcro, cork, felt, and so forth, can be used for tactile vari-ety on teacher-made worksheets.

- Use scented or tactile stickers for your student's papers; braille label tape can be used for grades or short comments.
- Manipulatives that are color-coded can be made tactile-coded with the addition of self-stick textures. The best manipulatives are the ones that will stay together (such as Unifix Cubes).

You might want to get the following items for your classroom. Check with the TVI to see if he/she can provide them.

- Braille/large print Dolch word cards, braille phonics practice sheets, heavy line writing paper, Franklin talking dictionary
- Braille/large print math flashcards, raised-line/heavy-line graph paper, braille/large print ruler, tactile protractor and compass, tactile learning clock, talking scientific calculator, tactile basic geometry kit
- Tactile land forms, tactile globe, braille and relief maps
- Raised-line anatomical drawings
- Sight, sound, and touch art books
- Braille large print playing cards, bingo, Uno, Connect Four, Monopoly, tic-tac-toe, tactile dice, bell balls, beep balls
- Braille or talking watch, talking clock, large print or tactile timer

Ask your student's TVI to suggest other special items that could enhance your student's learning. Many commercially available items can also be used successfully with blind/VI students.

THE CHILD WITH ADDITIONAL DISABILITIES: SOME CONSIDERATIONS

The blind/VI child may have disabilities in addition to his/her eye condition. This can present a challenge to educators. The child's visual disability might fall anywhere along the continuum from visual impairment to total blindness; additional disabilities could be cognitive, physical, neurological, medical, and so on, and could range in each of these areas from mild to severe. A child, for example, might be totally blind and have autism, or be partially sighted with a learning disability, or partially sighted, medically fragile, and severely retarded. The possible combinations are endless.

It can be difficult for those new to blindness/visual impairment to sort out whether delays or learning difficulties are due to the visual impairment or due to other disabilities. Typically, the assumption is that they are due to blindness/visual impairment. For example, if a child is not talking at age 2 and a-half, it is typical for parents, doctors, and teachers (though not teachers of the visually impaired) to assume that the delay in speech is due to the blindness/visual impairment. It is easy to make this assumption—it seems obvious that blindness/visual impairment would be the cause. But this assumption is often wrong! It is very important for the team to learn about the typical development of blind/VI children so that any additional conditions the student might have can be addressed and appropriate intervention begun without delay.

A Positive Approach

Regardless of what combination of eye condition and other disabilities your student has, the philosophy remains the same. Be positive; have a can-do attitude; keep expectations high. Blind/VI students are already at risk for lowered expectations on the part of the adults in their lives; those with additional disabilities are even more so. Don't make negative assumptions, even about the most involved child. Don't close doors; keep them open.

The approach to teaching presented throughout this book applies to the child with additional disabilities, too. Identify the student's needs in developmental, functional, and academic areas, based on his or her cognitive or learning profile, not based on blindness/visual impairment. Decide what will be taught. Add in the adaptations, materials, and techniques for blindness/visual impairment. Make sure that both student and teachers receive adequate training in special equipment and techniques from the TVI. Have special materials ready. Involve the parents who know their child very well and can tell you what works in terms of behavior, motivation, communication, and so forth.

Many blind/VI students with additional disabilities will learn to read and write, to travel with a cane, and to use a computer. The presence of additional disabilities in a blind/VI person does not foreclose the possibility of learning such skills. Again, the decision to teach academic skills, functional skills, developmental skills, or some combination of these should be made on the basis of the student's whole learning profile, not on the basis of blindness/visual impairment alone.

You Already Know

If you have taught children with various disabilities before, you will find that many, if not most, of the items in your bag of tricks will work with your blind/VI student, too. Often it is just the materials or the presentation of materials that will differ, for example, using a real apple instead of a picture of an apple. Think about what you would do in various situations if your student were not blind/VI. How would you get the child's attention? How would you redirect behavior? What expectations would you have? What activities would you try? What behaviors would you expect? Just add the adaptations for blindness/visual impairment in terms of materials and presentation to what you already know how to do.

Your student would likely also benefit from the same sorts of formal interventions that you would try with a sighted child with a similar learning picture, for example, sensory integration therapy, dance/movement training, music therapy, hippotherapy, social skills sessions, and so forth.

The Goal of Independence for the Child with Additional Disabilities

Full independence in the classroom and in later life may not be a reasonable goal for some children with additional disabilities, but teachers should still work toward the most independence the student can possibly achieve. Removing the aide from the classroom may not work for some students with additional disabilities, but the aide should still step back whenever the student can participate independently or with classmates.

Active not Passive

The blind/VI child with multiple disabilities is at great risk of being handled, moved, manipulated, and maneuvered by the adults in his/her life. Purposeful, self-initiated, independent movement is just as important for this child as it is for the child with no additional disabilities. This student has the same need for making choices, taking action, and having some control over the environment as any other student. Do not inadvertently encourage your student to be passive rather than active. Be sure to allow your blind/VI student with additional disabilities no less autonomy than you allow your sighted students with similar cognitive profiles.

Troubleshooting

All children, including those with severe disabilities, have a personality. In addition, there will be days when they are happy and days when they are grumpy, days when they feel well and full of energy, and days when they are dragging. Allow your student the freedom (within reason, naturally) to express his/her personality and feelings. Don't make it an IEP goal for the child always to be cooperative during therapies or manipulations. Use *your* gifts and tricks to motivate the student and make him/her *want* to participate.

Communication

The blind/VI student who cannot communicate with words may use various sounds, movements, and cries in order to get your attention or respond to what is going on. In addition to using all the ways you already know to evoke a positive response in a student, by all means ask the parents what works at home—to motivate or calm the child, to make the child happy or evoke a laugh, to stimulate the child to move, make sounds, take action, and so on. Make sure you find out how the child communicates that something is wrong.

When you understand what various sounds, head and body movements, and hand gestures might mean, you can be responsive to the student and he/she can feel some sense of control over the environment. Be alert to all efforts the child makes at communication, be they movements, signs, gestures, noises. Pay close attention so that the child's true potential does not remain hidden.

Might your student be able to use an augmentative communication device? These devices can be adapted for blindness/visual impairment by adding real objects, simple pictures, self-stick textures, large print, braille, and the like.

Troubleshooting

Some children may writhe, moan, cry, or scream during activities. Don't necessarily interpret this as the child's not being cooperative. It may simply be the only way this child has to communicate. Although the noises may be disturbing, don't punish the child for communicating and don't squelch communication. Again, check with the parents to see what the various movements and sounds might mean.

Be careful not to invade the child's personal space. Give the student some notice of your arrival and of what is about to happen or what you are about to do. Ask permission or at least let the child know when you are going to touch him or her. Use caution with the hand-over-hand technique. If your student is using his/her hands to see, hand-over-hand could feel to the child like getting poked in the eye.

Alternative Techniques and Materials

In order to engage the student and help him/her attend to and enjoy an activity, try these adaptations for blindness/visual impairment. Make it bigger, slow it down, give it contrast. Add sound, add echo, add reverberation, add vibration. Include taste, include smell. Use real objects. Add large print, add braille. Make it sparkly, make it shiny, light it up. Make it smooth, make it silky, make it velvety. Make it clinky, make it clattery. All these can be motivators for the blind/VI child to pay attention, to touch, to take action.

Other standard methods for engaging the student will work with your blind/VI student, too, such as offering rewards and pairing new learning with an activity you know the child enjoys.

A word of warning—make sure the sights, sounds, and textures you use do not overwhelm the child. Check with the parents to ensure that the child's response is one of enjoyment rather than of overload. Of course, you'll recognize it if the student shuts down.

The Active Learning Approach

A very exciting and successful approach to the education of blind/VI children with significant additional disabilities is the Active Learning approach of Dr. Lilli Nielsen. Dr. Nielsen, who has more than 30 years of experience working with blind/VI children, has written extensively on the subject, created many wonderful materials, and developed a comprehensive curriculum that can be used in the classroom and in the home. (Please see Resources, page 204.) Active learning works with even the most significantly delayed and disabled children, enabling them to learn that they can act upon the world and initiate interaction with others.

Picture a child in a prone position being supported comfortably under her chest and tummy by a little bolster or wedge. The child's hands just touch the surface below. The surface is a large wooden board with a rim around it raised a few inches off the floor. Under and around the child's hands is an array of objects—nesting measuring spoons, plastic cups, wooden beads, an electric toothbrush, a string of pearls. Every time the child makes even the slightest motion, her hands come in contact with some object or other, and even the slightest movement of the object makes a significant and pleasant noise on the wooden board.

The child quiets the first few times her hand comes in contact with an object and the noise occurs. Then she unconsciously flails her hands a bit in reaction to the noise. This results in an even better noise. The child laughs. Before you know it, the child is purposely trying to move her hands to touch the objects. She has learned that she can make something pleasing happen herself. This is the essence of Active Learning.

Created for children whose developmental age is 3 and a-half years or younger, the Active Learning approach enables the child with multiple disabilities to learn in the same way that very young children without disabilities learn—by doing, rather than by being trained or taught. In this approach the child is provided with opportunities to learn through active exploration and examination of specially created environments. Teachers (and parents) set up developmentally appropriate environments full of interesting objects that encourage the child to touch, move, learn, and explore. They then respond to the child's actions and sounds and interact with the child at his/her level of interest and development.

Some teachers have used Lilli Nielsen's approach within their class-rooms, setting up appropriate, stimulating environments and allowing stretches of time long enough for the student to explore, discover, and enjoy the objects, sound, textures, and movements. Teachers report that the sighted children in the class enjoy and benefit from this approach as well.

CHAPTER 8

ACCESSING THE CURRICULUM

Classroom Techniques and Subject Guide

In schools around the country, blind/visually impaired students are happily engaged in learning every subject in the curriculum. Some subjects require little or no adaptation in order for a blind/VI student to participate. Others take a little more creativity and effort. This chapter contains suggestions for the various subjects and for techniques teachers can use in the classroom to ensure that the blind/VI student has access to the material presented. Check the Resources chapter, page 187, for sources of specialty items mentioned.

CLASSROOM TECHNIQUES

Boardwork

- Verbalize what you are writing on the board, spelling out words and names when needed. Sometimes providing a desk copy of the material is appropriate, especially if the work includes drawings or diagrams.

Making It Work: Educating the Blind/VI Student in the Regular School, 103–122
Copyright © 2005 by Information Age Publishing
All rights of reproduction in any form reserved.

- To make your writing more visible, use high contrast colors (check with your student to see which colors work best), use print instead of cursive, leave space between lines, and keep the board clean. Allow the student to come up to the board to read.
- For assignments that are on the board at the beginning of class—
  - The student can come up to the board to read the assignment.
  - The teacher can read the assignment to the blind/VI student or can designate another student to read it to him/her; the blind/VI student can then do the assignment.
  - The teacher can write the assignment down or designate a student to write it; the blind/VI student can complete it and hand it in at a later time.
  - The blind/VI student can ask for the assignment and write it down; he/she can complete it then or at a later time.
  - Provide a desk copy for the student. If there is an aide or technical assistant (see page 144), the teacher can give him/her the assignment in advance for adapting; the teacher then gets it back from the assistant in braille or large print and gives it to the student.
- Electronic or interactive whiteboard technology enables you to send the information from the board to a laptop or PC monitor at the student's desk.

Handouts or Packets

- Give the handout to the aide or technical assistant in advance for brailling or enlarging. When you hand out the material to the class, give the adapted copy to the blind/VI student.
- If work has not been brailled or enlarged, give the student a regular print copy of the item. (The braille user needs a print copy of all assignments. The print copy should be stapled to the top of the braille copy.)
- See A Plan for Getting Materials Adapted, page 147.

Overhead/Projector Presentations

- Verbalize, spelling out words and names when needed.
- Provide a desk copy for the student. (Give the work to the technical assistant or aide beforehand for brailling or enlarging, as above).

Group Work

- For reading and writing feedback, instead of exchanging papers, students can read their own paper aloud to the others; students can take notes while others read and give feedback orally.
- Another option is for students to exchange computer files of their work. The blind/VI student can read a classmate's composition on the computer or on a notetaker and make notes and suggestions; sighted children can type in asterisks to indicate places where they've made suggestions or changed the blind/VI student's work.
- Some students are particularly good at working with a blind/VI student—they remember to say things aloud, enjoy describing what is happening, and so forth. If you have such students in the class, get them into the blind/VI student's group!
- If you are unsure of what parts of the group's work the blind/VI student can do, check with the TVI, the parents, and blind/VI adults for information and ideas. Create a situation in which the blind/VI student knows what to do in the group and how to do it; avoid a situation where the other students perceive the blind/VI student as a burden or where students feel the blind/VI student is not carrying his/her weight.
- If the blind/VI student is able to find partners and groups without difficulty, you won't need to intervene. If you notice that he/she is having trouble finding a partner or group to work with, however, you can facilitate by assigning students to groups or by more subtly suggesting who should work with whom. A way to avoid overusing a willing classmate is to note what skills the blind/VI student needs to develop in order to find partners or better participate in a group. Then make sure those needs get addressed.

Tests and Exams

- Give tests in advance to the aide or transcriber for brailling or enlarging. The blind/VI student can then take the test along with everyone else. If the student needs extra time to complete it, he/she can do so during the school day, after school, or at home for homework.
- In classrooms with an aide, the young blind/VI student often receives almost constant support. This support is then completely withdrawn during a test. To be fair to the student, make sure he/she

gets some practice working solo before he/she is expected to be able to do it in a test situation.

- Formatting issues can keep a student from performing at his/her best on tests (see Considerations for Evaluators, page 51, and Problems with Adapted Books, page 114). When this occurs, look for alternative ways in which the student can show you what he/she knows. For example, perhaps the TVI can redo certain sections or perhaps someone could read those sections to the student.

- If the test will include tactile illustrations or diagrams, make sure the student has seen the information presented in that same form before in practice materials (see Inconsistent Presentation, page 107).

- If the student is taking the test on a notetaker (see page 27), he/she can print out his/her answers during free time in the school day or after school and then hand in the print copy to the teacher. If the test is taken on a braillewriter, the TVI or aide who has learned braille can write in the print above each line of the student's braille and then give the test to the teacher for grading.

Quizzes

- If the quiz is ready in adapted form, the student can take it along with everyone else.

- If it is not in braille or enlarged, the student can take the quiz orally in one of the following ways:
  - Teacher reads the quiz aloud; student writes down answers.
  - With a reader (someone who reads print material aloud for a blind/VI person) in another room; reader reads the test to the student; student writes answers or the reader can mark answers on the print copy; student then gives the quiz to the teacher for grading. If student writes down own answers, he/she can then follow along when teacher goes over answers in class.
  - Student can take quiz home and do with a reader at home.

Videos

- The blind/VI student will use listening skills. The student may want to sit up close.

- The teacher or a classmate can describe important scenes that have no dialogue, if necessary to the understanding of the scene.

- Send the video home for preview.
- The video may be available with "audio description," a format in which a special narration is added to the soundtrack; the narration describes costumes, settings, facial expressions, movements, etc. that would not be visible to the blind/VI viewer. The narration is timed so that it does not interfere with the dialogue (see Resources, page 202).

Using Tactile Illustrations

Blind/VI students can benefit greatly from learning how to examine and extract information from tactile illustrations (see Interpreting Tactile Graphics, page 34). Tactile illustrations are not always usable, though, so teachers are cautioned not to go overboard with them. The following two additional problems that can occur with them are worth thinking over.

One-to-One Help
Occasionally, when a tactile illustration is very complicated or very different from the print original, the student might need some orientation to it or might even need one-to-one assistance in using it. Teachers must be sure not to let this kind of one-to-one assistance from an adult become a regular practice in the classroom for this or other purposes. It is at least as important for that student to be an independent participant in class and to interact normally with the other students, as it is for him/her to read that diagram!

Perhaps someone could go over the drawing with the student 5 minutes before class begins, during a study hall, or before or after school. Another alternative is to send the drawing home for preview. Look for creative solutions that will keep the blind/VI student involved with the class, not off to one side with an adult.

Inconsistent Presentation
Another area that can cause trouble for the blind/VI student is inconsistent presentation of concepts and materials. Sighted students see concepts illustrated in a consistent manner throughout their books, workbooks, worksheets, and test materials. Blind/VI students are usually not that lucky. They may see a concept presented in one way in their braille book, in another way on a practice sheet made by a technical assistant, in another way when mom or dad assists with homework at night, and in yet another way on a teacher-made test.

The concept may be barely recognizable as the same in all these differ-ent forms. We must make sure we are teaching and testing the student *on the ability to understand the concept and not on the ability to decipher drawings*. The issue of inconsistently done tactile drawings becomes critical on stan-dardized tests, since student placement often depends on test outcomes. Make every effort to use the same materials for teaching, practicing, and testing on a concept.

SUBJECT GUIDE

Reading

The most important consideration for a young blind/VI student learn-ing to read is that he/she has an efficient reading medium that supports the development of literacy skills and enables the child to keep up with the class. The next requirement is to have all the reading materials ready in accessible form when they are needed. If the materials are ready, the student will be able to participate in all aspects of the class.

The reading medium might be braille, large print, regular print, or a combination of these. The student might also use recorded material and a closed circuit television (CCTV) for certain reading tasks, but unless the student has a severe additional disability, neither recorded books nor a CCTV should be the primary reading medium. (For further discussion of this issue, please see The Skills and Tools of Blindness, page 23.) All ancil-lary materials, such as workbooks and practice sheets, should also be ready in the appropriate medium.

Reading Placement
Decisions about reading group placement for blind/VI students should be made on the same basis as for sighted students. The TVI can help you evaluate the student's comprehension of written material, vocabulary, ability to decode words, reading speed, and so forth. Don't make negative assumptions about the child's potential or ability to read based on blind-ness/visual impairment!

Making a good reading placement decision is especially important for the blind/VI student because of the time factor involved in obtaining accessible materials. If the student is moved to a new reading class or group that is using a different book, it might be difficult to obtain the book in an accessible format, since the braille or large print version usu-ally has to be ordered months in advance.

Reading Group

Here are some tips for success in reading groups:

- Teamwork and good communication between the classroom teacher and the TVI make it possible for the blind/VI student to be included in all reading and language arts activities. For the young braille user who is still learning the braille code, this usually means sharing lesson plans so that the TVI can introduce braille contractions to the student before they are needed for vocabulary in class.

- Although the pages in the braille version of a textbook will be keyed to the pages in the print original, the page turns in the braille book will probably be different from the print book. (Please also see About Braille Books, below.)

- Illustrations are usually omitted from the braille version of the book. Provide a few words of explanation if the pictures carry the plot.

- Facilitate independent participation by placing braille or large print volumes in a place convenient to the student.

- Ask the TVI to provide a braille cheat sheet (an alphabetical print listing of the braille letters, contractions, and punctuation marks) so that you can assist your student when necessary.

- If your student is using a fiction book recorded on tape, chapters may be indicated with a beep and page numbers may be read aloud, depending on whether the book was recorded as a textbook or as a leisure reading book. Books recorded as textbooks on CD have a *go to page* command.

- If the student's book is available on tape only, it will be difficult for him/her to look up and cite quotations from the book for book reports or papers. This would be a good time for the student to use a reader and a print copy of the book (please see Using Readers, page 35).

Other suggestions for optimizing the student's participation can be found in Specifics for Classroom Teachers, page 77.

About Braille Books

For a full discussion of braille textbooks, please see *The Bridge to Braille: Reading and School Success for the Young Blind Child* (Castellano & Kosman, 1997, listed in Resources, page 209). Following are some basics:

- The braille version of a textbook generally has more pages than the print version (the exception is storybooks for the youngest readers, where there are very few words on a page and the braille is transcribed page for page). Braille textbook pages are keyed to the page numbers in the print book; print page 27 may translate into braille pages 27, a 27, and b 27. Page turns will therefore be different for the braille user. Paragraphing, chapter breaks, headings, and so on will be the same.

- For longer books, the braille version will be separated into volumes. A print page at the beginning of each volume tells what pages are included in that volume.

- Glossaries appear in separate volumes at the end of the book, often called supplements.

- The student usually needs only one or two braille volumes of each textbook at his/her desk at a time; volumes not in use should be kept on a shelf or in boxes where the student has access to them, preferably in the classroom. The student will take home the volume/s needed for homework.

- Often, illustrations, charts, maps, diagrams, and so forth *will not be* in the braille book; figures in math books generally *are* included.

- The student will also need a print copy of every textbook.

About Recorded and Electronic Books

- Your student may get some textbooks on cassette tape or CD. These require special playback machines or software that allows access to the different tracks (in the case of tapes) and navigation capabilities (in the case of CDs).

- If the book was recorded on tape as a textbook (as opposed to as leisure reading), the page numbers will be read aloud on the recording; if the book was recorded as a leisure book, page numbers will not be announced.

- Textbooks recorded on tape generally have several cassettes.

- Electronic files of textbooks are increasingly available from publishers and other sources. The student can access these files on the computer screen, through computer speech, via paper braille, or on a computer or notetaker braille display. Please see Technology, page 164, for more information.

- Whatever medium the book is in, the blind/VI student will also need a print copy. Tapes can snag; technology can break down. The student still needs a way to get through the assignment! With a print copy, he/she can do the assignment with a reader.

About Large Print Books

- Large print books, too, can be separated into volumes. Store volumes not in use in a place where the student will have access to them so he/she can be independent in their use.
- The student needs a set of regular print textbooks, too. Sometimes parts of words or sentences are cut off or missing in the enlarged book. The student might prefer using the regular print book with a magnifier or a CCTV for mapwork (most of the pages in the large print book will be without color) or any tasks requiring measuring (please see Enlarging Illustrations, page 148).

Math

In order to successfully include a blind/VI student in math class, keep these tips in mind (items mentioned can be found in Resources, page 187):

- When presenting new concepts, give your young student plenty of opportunities to hold objects in his/her hands. Don't rely on the raised-line drawings in math books when presenting new concepts. Begin with concrete objects; then move on to their 2-dimensional representations. Older, more experienced students will probably be able to use the drawings in the book.
- Use manipulatives that will stay together, such as Unifix cubes. These can be texture-coded instead of color-coded with the addition of various self-stick textures (see Figure 8.1).
- Use a tray with raised edges or a box to hold manipulatives so that they will not fall off the desk when the child is working with them.
- A Dycem pad will keep manipulatives from sliding around.
- Tape a braille or large print number line on the student's desk to provide the same kind of reinforcement and reminders that sighted children get from looking at the number cards placed around the classroom.
- Use 3-D objects when first teaching about geometric shapes.
- When the student is able to understand 2-D representations, instead of using raised-line drawings, cut the shapes out and let the child examine them in his/her hands. Use lightweight cardboard

Figure 8.1.   Texture-coded math manipulatives.

(the kind used for the backing of a pad of paper works well) instead of paper. Holding the cardboard shapes will enable the student to perceive the contours of the shapes better.

- For folding to show symmetry and the like, use very lightweight cardboard (the kind used to package a men's dress shirt or a pair of stockings works well).
- You can make quick raised-line drawings with a coloring screen.
- Teach, give practice, and test your student on the same adapted materials. If you make an adapted item to use with your student, chances are it will vary from the way the concept is presented in his/her textbook. The child might see yet another presentation on the test. Inconsistent presentation of concepts can make it very difficult for the student to solidly learn a concept—so *teach, give practice, and test on the same materials!*
- Many math aids for use with blind/VI students exist, such as large print and braille flashcards; raised-line and heavy-line graph paper; braille and large print rulers, meter sticks, measuring tapes, compasses, and protractors; a raised-line geometry kit; and talking and large print calculators. Ask the TVI and check the catalogs for more items.

- Give your student lots of practice reading charts and graphs so that when these come up on standardized tests, he/she will be able to handle them. Your student can create graphs by drawing them or using braille or by using self-stick textures on raised-line graph paper.
- Some students are taught to do math using special equipment made for the blind, such as an abacus, on which they work the problem. Your student may or may not be taught these methods by the TVI; it will depend on whether or not your school district emphasizes the process of math thinking and wants to see each step of the work written out.

Doing Math in Braille

Braille users learn to do math using Nemeth Code, the system of writing mathematical notation in braille. Any mathematical problem, even the most complex, can be written in Nemeth Code, which enables braille users to take algebra, geometry, calculus, and any other advanced math course they desire. Nemeth Code is very precise—there is an exact layout and spacing for each kind of problem or equation. Nemeth Code cheat sheets are available to help you guide your student. Usually only a certified braille transcriber or a TVI has the expertise to create math papers in braille.

In the early grades most sighted students write the answers to math problems onto workbook pages and do not write out the whole example. Young braille users, however, are usually taught to write out the whole problem because it is not easy to write the answers in braille on the braille workbook page. For this reason, it often takes the young braille user extra time to complete math assignments. While it might seem like a good idea to assign fewer problems to the braille user, it is actually a better idea to make sure that the student learns efficient methods for setting up math problems, gets plenty of practice, and learns how to work up to speed. (For an in-depth discussion of doing math in braille, please get hold of *The Bridge to Braille: Reading and School Success for the Young Blind Child,* listed in Resources, page 209.)

Troubleshooting

Too many blind/VI students fall behind in math in the primary grades. Sometimes this occurs because the student has trouble seeing the problems (the plus sign [+] and the divided by sign [÷] can look alike) or cannot read his/her own writing. (That student probably needs braille.) Sometimes it happens because the child has experienced delays in development. Sometimes it is because the book moves quickly from topic to topic and the student doesn't get enough time to practice. Sometimes it occurs because of problems in the braille or enlarged book (please see below). Whatever the reason, the student who does not master basic concepts and skills in the first, second, and third grades is almost destined not to be able to move on to algebra and geometry in later years.

It might take extra effort to keep your student on grade level. Here are some techniques to try:

- Put something that illustrates the concept into the child's hands. For example, tactily-coded Unifix cubes can demonstrate the concept of a whole being divided into equal parts.

- If you are using a textbook that briefly touches on various topics and then revisits the topics in later chapters, you probably expect your students to have familiarity with concepts and methods of working problems when the topic is next visited. In order for your blind/VI student to gain such familiarity, try the following:

  ▪ Have all adapted materials ready so that the student has a chance to do each problem and participate in each part of the activity.

  ▪ Make sure the student gets time to practice the skills. Maybe the parents could give the child some extra practice at home.

  ▪ If you feel you must cut back on the child's workload, it might make sense to cut back on another assignment and have the student complete the math.

Problems with Adapted Books

Sometimes the raised illustrations in braille math textbooks are not usable—right angles are not drawn at 90°, squares are not really square, figures are out of proportion. Sometimes the caption or key is several pages away from the illustration it belongs with. Frequently concepts are illustrated inconsistently, being shown with one raised-line pattern on one page and a completely different pattern on another page, making it impossible for the student to recognize it as the same concept. This can make life difficult for the blind/VI student! If you are aware of these potential problems, you can check the drawings and provide assistance to your student when necessary.

Formatting is another issue that can cause problems for the student in the braille version of math textbooks. Although guidelines exist for the transcription of braille math books, those who transcribe the books also use their own judgment in many cases. Sometimes the concept being presented is simply not accessible to the student through what is shown on the braille page. If you are aware of this potential problem, you can work with the TVI to find other ways to present the material to the blind/VI student.

Beware of tasks in the book requiring measuring! In both braille and large print books, the figures are often drawn or blown up out of scale to each other or to the ruler (either a real one or the one given in the book). This phenomenon occurs on standardized tests, as well. The blind/VI student can certainly learn to measure, but to do it, he/she needs usable, accurate materials. In order to complete measuring assignments correctly, large print users often prefer to use the standard print book with a magnifier for these tasks. An adapted item in the correct scale may have to be made for the braille user.

As you correct papers, keep this in mind: if you are pretty sure the student understands the concept, but he/she has gotten various problems wrong, check to see if there are problems with the illustrations or formatting in the book.

World Languages

The same basic adaptations for group work, boardwork, handouts, screen presentations, tests and quizzes, videos, etc. listed in the Classroom Techniques section (page 103) will work for world languages. Here are some additional tips:

- When vocabulary is introduced through pictures and your student cannot use pictures, give the student the English word or phrase in place of the picture; for example, if the picture shows a tennis racket, just write *tennis* in English; if the scene shows the grandmother cooking, simply write *Grandma cooks* in English. The student can then write the answers in the language being learned.

- Have the vocabulary words and phrases that appear on posters and signs around the classroom put into braille or large print for the student to keep in a folder.

- When students are asked to draw, the blind/VI student can create a word picture instead.

- To make a map of the country, please see Three Ideas for Tactile Maps, page 156.

Science

Make sure your student gets every opportunity to participate fully in science activities. Encourage your student to observe nature and to touch everything. Support the blind/VI student with a serious interest in science, just as you would a fully sighted student. Encourage him/her to read books about science, take math courses, and pursue a career in science. There are blind/VI biologists, chemists, physicists, astronomers, and so forth who can serve as role models for your student, and special summer programs in which blind/VI students can participate. In addition, more and more tactile tools are being developed to aid blind/VI students in studying science (see Resources, page 193).

The suggestions for group work, boardwork, handouts, screen presentations, tests and quizzes, videos, and so on given in the Classroom Techniques section (page 103) are all appropriate for science class. Here are some additional tips:

- Give the student a hands-on or close-up view of what's going on. Seat the student near your desk or near where you like to stand when giving demonstrations so that you can place each object on the student's desk.
- Verbalize what is happening.
- Whenever possible, show the student lab equipment in advance so he/she can visualize what is going on during the lab.
- Before or after class, let the student handle test tubes, beakers, graduated cylinders, balances, stands, and other apparatus. Have him/her practice pouring and mixing, using water. Have him/her examine a Bunsen burner and a hot plate. Show your student a microscope so that he/she can learn its parts and functions, even though he/she may not use it to explore things visually.
- Have the blind/VI student work with a partner. The partner can describe his/her observations for things that cannot be touched. The blind/VI student can read the steps of the lab, do various parts of the lab, keep time, takes notes, and so forth.
- For complex illustrations that your student cannot access, the teacher can tape record an explanation, bringing out the points he/she wishes to emphasize. Caution—this must be done by a teacher who knows the subject, not by an aide!
- If you make a model or raised-line drawing for your student, make sure you teach, give practice, and test on the same model. If the concept is shown in completely different ways in the textbook, practice materials, and test, it may not be recognizable as the same concept.

Social Studies

The suggestions for group work, boardwork, handouts, screen presentations, tests and quizzes, videos, and so forth, given in the Classroom

Techniques section (page 103) are applicable to social studies class. Here are additional suggestions:

- For mapwork in a book that has been enlarged, make sure the scale has been enlarged to the same percentage as the map! If you feel the student understands the concept, but keeps getting map questions wrong, check to see if this is the problem. Your student might prefer to use a regular print book with a magnifier for mapwork.
- Your student might benefit from viewing maps and illustrations with a CCTV, especially if it has a color monitor.
- If your student does not have access to a map, he/she can learn the information through verbal description instead. This can work for illustrations and charts, too.
- Check Three Ideas for Tactile Maps, page 156.
- Social studies class is often a good time for a student to begin learning to use a reader (please see Using Readers, page 35). For example, if the student needs to get information from a very complicated chart that would be unwieldy to enlarge or transcribe into braille, he/she could use a reader to access the chart.
- NFB Newsline for the Blind provides access to daily newspapers and several magazines via the telephone. See Resources, page 191, for details.

Physical Education

Participation in physical activity during childhood leads to many rewards—physical fitness and good health, enjoyment of games and sporting events, interaction with peers, lifelong participation in sports and fitness activities. The blind/VI child needs and deserves to participate in vigorous physical activity just like any other child. Make sure your blind/VI student is not just sitting on the bench!

Many athletic blind/VI people participate in sports and games at the local, state, national, and even international competition levels in just about every sport you can think of. There is also a special game created for the blind/VI called goalball. Encourage your student to check into opportunities in the community to participate in sports.

The blind/VI student does not need a special gym class; he/she can be integrated into a regular class. (Please see Make It Successful for Every Child, page 178.) All that's needed are a few adaptations and a teacher willing to ask the question, "How can we get a blind kid into this game?" Here are some of the ways:

- Get a key lock or push button lock instead of a combination lock for the student's locker.
- For the partially sighted student, it generally helps to slow the action down, make the ball or target bigger, and make use of contrast.
- Use yellow gaffer's tape to delineate various areas.
- Add a sound cue to a target.
- Bell balls, beeper balls, bead jumpropes, and many other pieces of useful equipment are available.
- The student can walk/run/move toward a sound source such as a voice, clapping, or a beeper.
- Demonstrate the movements for an exercise or sport skill by moving the blind/VI student through the motions. (Ask the student's permission. The older student might feel embarrassed at being put on display.)
- The blind/VI student can also imitate your motions by touching your arm or leg as you demonstrate a movement. Imitation is not solely a visual skill.
- Teach your student the body mechanics for skills such as throwing, batting, passing, kicking, et cetera.
- Show the student the big picture of a game or ball field. Use a game board and pieces to show a baseball field and where the players line up; use a rectangle of cardboard and strips of Wikki Stix to make a football or soccer field, basketball court, etc.
- Not every blind/VI child will be interested in athletics or good at sports, but they should still have a general understanding of the concepts and rules of sports and games commonly played, just like their classmates. Ask the student what he/she already knows about the sport and then fill in any missing information.
- Encourage or assign willing classmates to partner with the blind/VI student during activities such as running and ball games. Make sure the student is not always with an aide.
- Describe the action of the game.
- The student can be the server for volleyball and can inbound for both teams for basketball and soccer.
- There are ways to include a blind/VI student in virtually any physical activity. Check the Sports, Games, and Leisure Time section of www.blindchildren.org for more ideas.
- Check to see if there is a division of the Association of Blind Athletes in your state (see Resources, page 202).

Health

Blind/VI students certainly need all the information taught in health classes. The suggestions given in the Classroom Techniques section (page 103) on including the blind/VI student in group work, boardwork, handouts, screen presentations, tests and quizzes, videos, and so forth, will help health class run smoothly. Here are a few more suggestions:

- For complex diagrams, the teacher could record a description emphasizing the important points or verbalize the description to the student who could take notes on the information.
- Raised-line anatomy drawings are available, as are accessible books on health and maturation issues.
- Models of male and female anatomy may be available from the TVI. It is wise to use models with a trusted adult in a private setting rather than in class.

Driver Education

Driver's Ed? For a blind/VI student? Yes, a blind/VI student, too, should be a part of what everyone else is learning. Driving is an enormous part of the teen years and the blind/VI student needs to be able to talk with friends about the process. Although he or she will not drive a car, that blind/VI teenager might well *own* a car as an adult. He/she also may have teens of his/her own some day and will want to have this information. In addition, in many places knowing the rules of the road is part of cultural competency.

Library

The blind/VI student should be included in all lessons concerning use of the library. Although the student might not access library materials directly, he/she needs to understand the setup of a library and how exactly to access materials so that he/she can direct a reader (please see Using Readers, page 35) and go on to be successful in higher education. Here are some tips:

- Make braille or large print copies of all practice materials so that the student can follow along during lessons.
- If the library computers are not accessible, have the student practice directing a reader to find information.
- For the younger student, label a few library shelves with braille or large print. To give your student some experience in choosing

books, order books from your state or regional library for the blind (see Resources, page 198), and place them on the labeled shelves.

Art

Blind/VI students enjoy expressing themselves through art as do sighted students. Although sculpture and 3-D art are natural media to explore, students also enjoy collage, painting, printmaking, and so forth. In addition, it is just as important for blind/VI students as for sighted students to have exposure to concepts such as symmetry, perspective, and the elements of composition, and the characteristics of the various periods of art history for their own cultural knowledge. Art Education for the Blind (see Resources, page 194) has produced some fabulous resources.

Here are a few tips:

- For young students, have materials precut and ready to use so that the student can participate in projects.
- Your student might enjoy working with Wikki Stix.
- Allow your student to choose which colors to work with. Teach commonly agreed upon color concepts—grass is green, the sky is blue, etc. Your student can then choose the conventional color scheme or can choose other colors to be creative or different or funny.
- Your student may enjoy painting with his/her hand held right on the bristle part of the paintbrush. Fingerpainting, of course, would be fun, too. Sand added to paint gives extra texture.
- Use raised-line outlines. These can be made with a tracing wheel, coloring screen, puffy paint, glue, or Wikki Stix.
- For folding activities, lightweight cardboard or heavyweight paper such as braille paper, will probably work better than regular paper.
- To demonstrate symmetry or other concepts, cut out shapes from lightweight cardboard for the student to examine and use. Lightweight cardboard works much better than paper for enabling the student to perceive the edges and contours.
- The student can examine art prints and the work of fellow students using a CCTV.

Music

Teachers usually have no trouble including a blind/VI student in music class. Here are a few tips:

- Braille or enlarge the words to songs for the student.
- Many teachers create feelable versions of the signs of musical notation—notes, rests, clefs, and so forth—to give the student an understanding of print music.
- Although many blind/VI students learn music by ear, many also want to learn to read music. Please see Resources, pages 192 and 193, for sources of braille or large print music.
- Your student can take the stage and climb onto risers. He/she may want to walk along with a classmate to get into position. While standing on the risers, the cane user can hold the cane straight up and down, leaning against one shoulder.
- Teach your blind/VI student how to get into the proper position on the risers, when to sit and stand, how to take a bow, and so forth.
- You might need to get creative in order to work out signals for cueing the student who cannot see your signals.

Home Economics

Blind/VI adults use many safe, efficient, nonvisual techniques for cooking and sewing tasks. Here are a few suggestions for the classroom:

- Label drawers and cabinets with braille or large print.
- A blind/VI rehabilitation teacher may be available to come to the school to consult and make suggestions.
- Hand-on experience is always best for your blind/VI student. Whenever possible, allow the student to handle ingredients and changing textures as ingredients are added and mixed.
- Tools and equipment of use to the blind/VI cook are available. The TVI may be able to provide them or check Resources, page 199.

Computer

Blind/VI people use computers for the same tasks that sighted people use them for—word processing, email, going online, and so forth. You will need to equip at least one computer at your school with adaptive software such as screen enlargement or speech for your student's use. The student who cannot see the screen will use keyboard commands instead of the mouse. It will be trickier to include this student in instruction during the regular computer class. It might prove more efficient and useful for the student to receive individual instruction from a specialist in adaptive computer technology before or during regular computer class time. Please see Technology, page 161, for further information on adaptive technology.

Shop

Believe it or not, safe, efficient methods exist for blind/VI people to run shop equipment. Rehabilitation centers around the country regularly teach such techniques. For information on methods for including a blind/ VI student in shop class, please contact the National Center for the Blind at 410-659-9413.

CHAPTER 9

THE ROLE OF THE
TEACHER'S AIDE

A teacher's aide can truly enhance a blind/visually impaired child's educational experience, especially when he/she understands the goal of independence. An aide can help ensure that the student gains a firm understanding of basic concepts, experiences, and situations and is not missing important chunks of information. If the blind/VI student's foundation is solid, then he/she will be able to learn more complicated material in later years without (or with very little) assistance. In addition, an aide can help the blind/VI child progress in the skills of blindness/visual impairment which will enable the student to work and move about independently.

Must there be an aide? An aide is not a necessity in every classroom that has a blind/VI student. In fact, if the blind/VI student is functioning independently, there *should not be* an aide involved. In such cases, the aide could become the technical assistant who works only in the background—adapting materials, enlarging books, creating braille, and so forth. For a discussion of this transition, please see page 144.

Many times schools are tempted to hire an aide primarily for safety reasons or to protect the blind/VI student. While the aide would provide some protection and monitoring of the very young student, the student must be allowed to develop the independent movement and safety skills that will enable him/her to protect and monitor him/herself. The development of these skills is a process; as the student gains skill, the aide can

Making It Work: Educating the Blind/VI Student in the Regular School, 123–145
Copyright © 2005 by Information Age Publishing

and must step back. The goal is for the blind/VI student to take as much responsibility for his/her own movement as a sighted child.

If it is determined that an aide is needed, a good want ad might read:

> Creative, upbeat, organized person needed to help adapt materials and assist in classroom with blind/VI student. Computer literate. Willing to learn braille. Some artistic ability a plus.

Most of the suggestions in this chapter pertain to the young blind/VI student, but they would also be useful for older students with delays. In general, very intensive involvement by an aide would no longer be appropriate for the older student. For the student who is on grade level, mid-third grade is a good target for eliminating direct assistance by the aide (or earlier, if the student is ready). Remember, however, that blind/VI students are vulnerable to falling behind, not due to lack of ability, but due to lack of access to materials, inadequate presentation of materials and concepts, and not enough in-the-hands experiences.

The Aide Who Is Assisting a Braille User

When classroom teachers and aides see a braille page for the first time, all they may perceive is a jumble of dots. It is necessary for someone in the classroom to be able to make sense of those dots and that person is usually the aide. The aide who will be assisting a young braille user needs to learn braille. The aide does not have to become an expert in the code; but he/she must learn enough to make sure that braille pages are situated correctly for the beginning student and are not upside down, to write in the print above the student's braille lines so that the teacher can correct the work, to find page numbers, to help a student stuck on a word, and to check for errors that sometimes occur in the braille version of textbooks. In addition, the TVI might ask the aide to provide follow-up between braille lessons.

Learning the basics of braille is fun and easy (and it doesn't take too much effort to stay a few steps ahead of a first-grader). Many school districts pay for the aide to take a short course in braille, perhaps taught by a TVI or a braille transcriber. There are several online courses offered (search learn braille). Courses leading to actual certification as a braille transcriber are available from the National Library Service (see Resources, page 198). These courses can be taken locally or by correspondence and provided are free of charge. The NLS directory *Sources of Custom-Produced Books: Braille, Audio Recordings, and Large Print* lists local braille transcribing groups that sponsor courses.

THE FUNCTIONS OF THE AIDE

The various functions of an aide can be divided into four general categories:

- Behind-the-scenes work;
- Direct assistance;
- Facilitating; and
- Enrichment.

Behind-the-Scenes Work

The behind-the-scenes work is probably the most important work a teacher's aide can do. It consists of the background planning and activity that sets the stage for the child to function independently in the classroom. The behind-the-scenes work is automatically done for sighted children so that they can perform at their best. For example, desks are designed so that books and pencils fit and can be put in logical places. Books, manipulatives, and other learning tools are all ready on the first day of school. Diagrams, maps, and charts are included in their books in usable formats. Posters and bulletin boards in the classroom provide additional learning opportunities. We can consider all of this as behind-the-scenes work for the sighted student.

The behind-the-scenes work for the blind/VI student serves to set up an equivalent learning environment. If the behind-the-scenes work is done with forethought and care, the child will be able to participate on an equal footing with sighted classmates and will have the opportunity to learn all of the concepts and skills presented. Here are some specifics:

- **Set up the desk area for maximum independence and organization (see Figure 9.1).**   The blind/VI student needs to know where his/her books will be kept, where extra paper will be, where to put completed work, where any special items will be, and so forth. Items should be within the child's easy reach. Arrange the space so that the child can find, use, and return items without help from an adult. Orient the child to the space if necessary. Rethink and change the desk set up when needed as the child progresses. Here are some organization ideas:
  - Purchase or make oversize folders that can accommodate enlarged pages or braille sheets; label folders in large print or braille. Place the braille label along the left edge of the front

cover in the same place the title of a braille book would appear, so that the child can simply reach out, read the title, and grab the needed folder.

- Vertical snap-together bins from an office supply store can be placed on the child's desk to organize and hold books and folders.

- Braille textbooks are separated into volumes. Place the current volume of each braille textbook at the child's desk and store the others in a convenient location. As the student gets older and more experienced, he/she will take over the task of getting the next volume from the storage place when it is needed. Avoid squirreling the books away behind desks or in other hard to reach locations.

- Make sure special supplies, such as Wikki Stix, tactile dice, braille labels, and so forth, are ready for the child's use and in logical places where he/she can reach them easily.

- *Remember, the desk must be set up for the child's use, not the aide's!* If the aide has a desk in the room, it should be in another part of the room, not next to the blind/VI child's desk. If the aide sits next to the student, others in the class will tend to view the blind/VI student as belonging to the aide, and not to the class. When the desks are separated, and the blind/VI student is seated among the other children, the teacher and the other children view the blind/VI child as a real part of the class. This arrangement helps the blind/VI student learn to focus on the teacher and not on the aide and also encourages social interaction.

- **Continually re-evaluate the classroom scene to keep pace with the child's progress.**   Identify tasks that are being done for the child which the child could begin doing for him/herself.

- **Keep track of any special items that come in.**   The TVI will order many special materials that help make the education of the blind/VI student a success. If you learn the uses of these materials and know where they are, you can make sure they are available when they are needed.

- **Coordinate and plan in advance with the classroom teacher and the TVI.**   Regular meetings will ensure that you have time to adapt materials in advance (see page 147). This way the materials will be ready when the teacher teaches that lesson.

- **Organize braille or enlarged worksheets in advance and give them to the teacher to hand out along with those for the other students.**   It is important that the teacher be the one to hand out

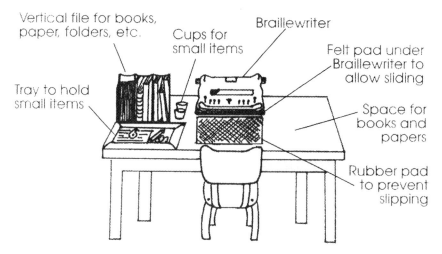

Vertical file for books, paper, folders, etc.

Cups for small items

Braillewriter

Felt pad under Braillewriter to allow sliding

Tray to hold small items

Space for books and papers

Rubber pad to prevent slipping

Figure 9.1.   Sample desk set up for maximum independence.

papers to the blind/VI student when he/she hands them out to the rest of the students in the class. This helps everyone remember that the blind/VI student is a real member of the class and not in a special class consisting of the aide and the blind/VI student.

- **Adapt materials for classroom subjects as well as for specials, such as music, world languages, and art.**   (See Adapting Materials, page 147.) Collect real objects and materials useful for adapting, such as cardboard, colored glue, Wikki Stix, markers, braille labeler, various self-stick textures, drafting taping, tracing wheel, and so forth (see Resources, page 187). On occasion, an adaptation for a lesson will consist of materials entirely different from what the other children will be using. Let the teacher know if this occurs and, if possible, orient the blind/VI child to the adapted item before class or ask the teacher to send it home for preview. It might be appropriate for you to show it to the blind/VI child during the lesson and unobtrusively supply information or instructions.
- **Check braille books to see if diagrams, charts, or maps were omitted (they often are).**   Sometimes, even when they are included, these illustrations do not work very well tactually. Check to see if the formats of brailled charts, and so forth make sense and are usable. Confer with the TVI and plan appropriate alternatives if needed (see Adapting Materials, page 151).
- **Collect any special materials or manipulatives required for the day's lessons.**   If the children change classes during the day, transport the necessary materials to the other rooms.

- **Staple a print copy on top of brailled worksheets.**   This makes for easy identification of the brailled sheet by the teacher, when he/she is going to hand out papers, and by parents, when sheets come home. Parents need a print copy so that they can see the assignments the child is working on and so that they can be as informed as the parents of sighted children in the class.

- **Transcribe the child's braille work by writing in the print above each line of braille.**   In the first few years of school, before the student has learned to use technology, it is extremely helpful if the aide can transcribe the child's brailled work. The blind/VI student should hand in the work to the teacher or place it in the designated spot, just like everyone else. Then the aide can retrieve it, write in the print, and return it to the teacher for correcting. This enables the teacher to correct and grade the blind/VI student's papers when he/she does the papers of the other children, without having to wait for the TVI to transcribe the work. Caution: if the aide writes in the print on the student's math papers, he/she must know the correct braille symbols for math, so that the child's work is transcribed correctly! Ask the TVI to check problems the student got wrong on math papers for possible transcription errors. In fact, it is a good idea for the TVI to check errors on all papers until the aide becomes proficient enough in braille.

- **Use a computer, braille embosser, and braille translation software to braille out items not transcribed by the TVI or transcribing service.**   Items such as worksheets, quizzes, last minute news articles, school announcements, report cards, programs for assemblies, the lunch menu, and so forth can all be put into braille for the blind/VI student. Having such items in accessible form helps the blind/VI student be a full participant in school.

- **Use a computer and braille embosser to braille out the teacher's comments and corrections.**   Double space between comments, then cut them apart and staple each one onto the child's paper next to the teacher's written comments. In this way, the blind/VI student gets feedback on schoolwork in the same manner as sighted classmates get it.

- **Use colored glue, bits of Wikki Stix, or other tactile materials to mark mistakes on papers that the teacher has graded.**   The blind/VI student can then look over his/her own papers, find the mistakes, and analyze them as others in the class do. Remember, it is the teacher who must correct and grade the blind/VI student's work, not the aide!

Over time, the nature of the behind-the-scenes work changes. For example, the older student will know how to print out his/her own work on a printer to hand in to the teacher, making it unnecessary to write in the print on braille papers. The junior high school student will no longer need corrections marked with a texture; he/she will ask the teacher or use a reader to review the teacher's comments. But this progress will only come to pass if the student has been given the opportunity to gain experience with a variety of learning materials and to build a strong base in grade level academics and blindness/visual impairment skills. It is up to the adults in the student's life to make sure that such opportunities are provided right from the start.

Direct Assistance

When people think of the function of an aide in a classroom with a blind/VI student, they most often picture the aide sitting at the child's side helping the child perform every task. *Helping the child* is the operative phrase in people's minds. While the child may indeed need assistance in the early years, it is crucial to *keep in mind the goal of independent participation* in school (and in life). The child must learn to do tasks for him/herself and should be expected to learn to do any task that is going to be repeated every day, such as opening milk cartons, placing homework papers in the homework basket, or standing properly to salute the flag.

The blind/VI student needs to learn how to listen to the teacher's instructions and then get going on the work. If an aide needs to intervene in the early years, this should be done unobtrusively and with a minimum of words, so that the student gets the idea that he/she needs to listen to the teacher. *At all times when the child is able to participate on his/her own, the aide should not interfere!*

What, then, is appropriate help? In general, appropriate help is the kind that *teaches* the skill. One way to think about this is to ask yourself, "Is the help I am giving the kind that will *teach* this student how to do the task on his/her own? Or am I doing the task *for* the child?" For example, putting the child's papers into the backpack at the end of the day is one form of help, but teaching the child how to pack the bag him/herself is a much better form of help.

Another useful way to judge the kind of help you are providing is to think about age appropriateness, or stage appropriateness for the child with additional disabilities. It might be appropriate for an aide to help a preschooler locate the hook in the cubby and hang up the backpack or to help with zipping up the child's jacket. However, this would no longer be appropriate for a fourth grader.

In the early years, an aide may have to help a student get through academic tasks. But, even then, the focus needs to be on teaching the child how to do these tasks independently, so that the aide's assistance is phased out as quickly as possible. Make sure that materials are ready and in logical places so that the student can get them without waiting for or depending on another person to get started. Only then will he/she be able to complete tasks from start to finish quickly and independently.

Other appropriate times for direct assistance might be in art class or physical education class. In phys ed, for instance, an aide could help a young blind/VI student locate a certain area of the gymnasium that is not tactually marked or could help the child participate in activities such as soccer or basketball. Even then, the aide should be as unobtrusive as possible and both aide and teacher should be alert at all times to ways to promote interaction between the blind/VI student and other students in the class. Again, in all cases, when the child is able to participate on his/her own, the aide should step back and not be involved. When an aide does directly assist a child physically, he/she should make sure he/she respects the child's personal space (see "My Body Belongs to Me," *Future Reflections*, Vol. 14, No. 3).

In general, if planning for independence is built in and if sufficient instruction and practice time is provided, less and less help will be needed as time goes on. From the beginning there should be a plan for the time when the aide will no longer be present. Again, for a young blind/VI student who is moving along academically and is on grade level, the target might be for the aide to be out of the classroom by the middle of third grade. (Of course, if the child can handle everything earlier than that, then withdrawing the aide earlier is fine!)

If the student is older, and you realize you probably should have worked on moving the aide out earlier, it can be helpful to think of the process in terms of weaning—weaning the child away from the aide (and in many cases, weaning the aide away from the child!). The student, especially the older student who has grown accustomed to a lot of help over many years, will probably need support during the weaning process. An abrupt severing of the relationship would probably be too severe. The older student who does not possess all of the necessary skills for independent functioning in the classroom will need to be taught the skills before he/she is set free.

Teaching a dependent student to function independently is something like teaching a child to ride a bike without training wheels. When we first take the training wheels off, we run alongside the bike, lightly holding the seat to keep the bike balanced. Before long, the child is able to balance the bike intermittently and we need to grab the seat only a few times each ride. Finally, the child gets the hang of riding alone and we no longer have to run alongside. The skills are in place. Give your blind/VI student lots of enthusiastic moral support as you back away and he/she learns the skills and takes those first steps toward independence.

Facilitating

Facilitating means bringing something about or making it easier for something to happen. In view of the goal of independence, facilitating for the blind/VI student means helping to bring about the student's independent functioning in the world as a skilled and competent blind/VI person. Facilitating therefore will work best when the aide has an understanding of the goal of independence, familiarity with the skills and tools of blindness/visual impairment, an overall sense of where the child is in the development of these skills, and an idea of what the next logical step would be.

There are many ways in which an aide can facilitate. Three of the most important are facilitating independent learning and functioning in the classroom, facilitating social interaction, and facilitating the child's independent mobility.

Facilitating Independent Participation in the Classroom

- **Encourage appropriate exploration.**   The young blind/VI child needs certain information in order to function independently. Guide the child *so the child can make discoveries* about the environment. Plan a few minutes every day—before or after school, or during a time when the classroom is empty—for some guided discovery. "Let's see what we find if we start at the doorway, turn left, and stay along the wall. Yes, that's the blackboard. Keep going. What do you see next? Yes, you've found the bookcase. And if you go along the bookcase, what happens next? Yes, the wall ends and we find a corner. Let's keep going. What do you see? Yes, there are the cubbies."

- **Promote the child's understanding of the classroom scene and how to respond appropriately.**   For example, while the child is learning to participate independently at circle time, you can sit a slight distance away from the child and discreetly whisper instructions if the child does not respond to the teacher on his or her own.

- **Give cues rather than help.**   For the blind/VI child who needs assistance, the sequence should be as follows: First, give help. Next, give training/practice. Next, give a cue to remind the child what to do. Next, teach the child to cue him/herself; instead of telling the child what to do, ask, "What should you do next?" Keep stepping back.

Facilitating Social Interaction (Also see page 90)

- **Give the child discreet feedback regarding appropriate postures and behaviors.**   For a variety of reasons, some blind/VI children do not position themselves correctly in situations such as facing the person talking, facing the flag, facing the center at circle time, and so forth. (If your student has a compromised visual field, he/she may not be able to see visual targets straight on and may need to tilt or turn his/her head; in this case, consult with the TVI.) In general, correct the blind/VI child the way you would a sighted child who was facing the wrong way or was otherwise situated incorrectly. If this remains an ongoing problem, it is possible to teach the child a "secret signal" to serve as a cue. For example, the word *face* could be whispered as a quiet reminder to the child to face the correct way. (Likewise, give the student a word of praise when things are going right, but be sure to do it when it won't interrupt his/her concentration on the teacher.)

   Other situations in which a secret signal would be useful are when the student holds his/her head down, presses a hand to his/her eye, or has some other habit considered socially unacceptable. You could use a snap of the fingers as a signal. A snap works well because it can be used discreetly from across a room without calling public attention to the child's habits.

- **Teach the blind/VI child what is expected in activities requiring partners.**   Some examples of this are cooperative learning activities in the classroom, square dancing in gym, or preparing for a concert or play. Again, the idea is to teach the child what he/she needs to know in order to participate independently. Once the child knows what to do, step back. If things are going fine, don't intervene.

- **Teach and remind sighted children (and adults) to identify themselves to the blind/VI child.**   "Hi, Sarah. It's Jennifer" or "Good morning, Sarah. It's Mrs. Smith." Absolutely discourage people from playing the "Do you know who this is?" game with the student. "Can you guess who this is?" or "Do you know my voice?" are the equivalent of coming up behind the back of a sighted person, slapping your hands over his/her eyes, and saying, "Guess who!" over and over again. This gets annoying pretty quickly!

- **Teach and remind the blind/VI child to ask the identity of those speaking to him/her.**   When someone says hello, the blind/VI child can respond, "Hi. Who's that?" This very useful skill will serve the blind/VI student through adulthood, since sighted people unaccustomed to blindness/visual impairment will usually not identify themselves first. The student might ask another child in line or at lunch, "Hi. Who's this in front of me?"

- **Promote social interaction and friendships.**   For a variety of reasons, some blind/VI students find it difficult to make friends and play with other children. You can help the child learn these skills by setting up play experiences in the classroom and on the playground. Initially, with younger children, you can be a part of the play, perhaps showing the blind/VI student what to do in various play situations and teaching the other children how to include the blind/VI child in play. As the blind/VI child gets the hang of social interaction, or if other children are effective at including the blind/VI child, step back. In the younger grades, an aide can be an attraction to the other children and can actually help bring others over to the blind/VI child. Very soon, however, the children form groups and do not need or want an adult involved, and an adult presence will actually impede social interaction for the blind/VI child. If you must remain involved in order for the blind/VI child to be included, be as unobtrusive as possible. If the interaction is moving along, disappear!

- **Give the blind/VI child information about what classmates are doing during recess times.**   The child needs to know the variety of play choices available both in the classroom and on the playground. Adapted games are available, too. Perhaps the TVI can supply braille/large print playing cards, Uno, Monopoly, Connect Four, and other adapted games (see Resources, page 187).

- **If necessary, teach the blind/VI child how to play the games that classmates are playing.**   Some blind/VI children have not learned how to play in typical ways and will not know what to do in play situations. If needed, teach appropriate responses to what other children say and do.

- **Work toward getting the blind/VI child into games.**   Teach the blind/VI child typical ways that children get into games. Be matter-of-fact about blindness/visual impairment. Teach everyone to think, "Let's figure out a way to get a blind/VI kid into this game." Many times simple adaptations can be made, like using a sound-making ball.

- **Teach the playground manners and protocols that children (and adults) expect everyone to follow.** For example, the blind/VI student, Sarah, has just gone down the slide. She walks around back to the ladder but a line has formed. Does she know she is supposed to go to the end of the line and wait her turn? Does she know how to find out where the end of the line is? Do the other children know they should call out and let her know where the end of the line is? (We don't want the blind/VI child to accidentally cut the line and have the other children resent her.) The aide can teach skills like this when the opportunity occurs naturally. "Sarah, there are five children in line. You need to find the end of the line and wait your turn. John, call out to Sarah so she knows where the end of the line is." Again, once the children get the hang of what to do, step back and let the blind/VI child join in with the others.

- **Teach the sighted children how to get the blind/VI child's attention.** "Jennifer, Mike can't see you waving your arm to him. If you want him to come over you need to say, 'Over here Mike, by the big swing set.'"

Facilitating Independent Mobility

- **Provide follow-up for mobility lessons.** Observe O&M lessons. Learn what cane techniques, routes, problem-solving skills, and so forth, the student is working on. Follow through when the mobility instructor is not there so that the student can practice and make progress in mobility skills every day.

- **Work toward the child's mastery of daily routes.** Each day will present opportunities for the student to practice the route to places he/she goes every day, such as other classrooms, the school office, the bathroom, the water fountain, the playground. First talk the child through the route. Next, follow at a close enough distance to give verbal cues if needed. Then watch from a distance. Don't always rush to help. Be sure to *allow time for independent problem-solving*. Finally, get out of the picture as soon as possible! The goal is for the child to move about within the school with the same degree of independence as sighted peers.

- **Work toward the student's mastery of cafeteria skills.** The student who buys lunch will need to learn how to move along in a line, handle a tray, deal with money, carry a tray while walking, and find a table. (Lunch is an important socialization time, so it is not necessarily a good idea simply to assign the blind/VI student to a nearby or convenient table or for the aide to sit with the child.) Consult with the O&M instructor and skilled blind/VI adults for ideas and tips on maneuvering in a crowded restaurant or cafeteria. If you notice that the child is having social difficulties at lunchtime due to poor manners or eating habits, gently let the parents know so that they can address these issues at home.

- **Don't lead the child around!**   It is imperative that the blind/VI student become *independent* in mobility. The technique of walking while holding on to someone else's arm (often called sighted guide) is overly prescribed by blindness professionals as a viable method of moving from place to place for the blind/VI student. The student who relies on this method will not develop independent mobility skills. This method must be used only sparingly, if at all.

Enrichment

A teacher's aide has the potential to greatly enrich the blind/VI student's educational experience. Enrichment activities enhance the blind/VI student's experience in meaningful and important ways and deepen the child's understanding and appreciation of lessons, events, and general goings on. Though enrichment generally occurs outside of class lesson times—before and after school, at less busy times during the school day, in the hallways, at special events, during school trips—it is no less necessary to the student's education. Enrichment is not *above and beyond*; enrichment is essential.

Here are some examples: Print books are full of photographs which illustrate many concepts. Whenever possible, provide real objects for the blind/VI child to examine, or mention the need to the classroom teacher, TVI, and family, one of whom might have access to the needed items. An aide might also notice an area in which the child lacks concepts or has incomplete information and could alert the teachers and family to this.

Another area in which an aide can provide enrichment is environmental print. The aide can ensure that the blind/VI student is exposed to the many concepts presented through the posters, bulletin boards, announcements, children's work, and so forth, that surround students in the classroom and in the halls. Once the student is aware that this kind of information exists, then he/she can begin learning how and when to obtain it for him/herself. He can begin to ask a classmate, "Alex, who's the new Student of the Month?" "Is there a new message on the principal's bulletin board?" "Have they posted next week's lunch menu yet?" "What's the word of the day for Spanish class?"

Providing verbal description is another example of enriching the blind/VI student's experience. During videos, school assemblies, and plays, the aide can unobtrusively and briefly explain what is happening if the meaning cannot be understood through words or dialogue alone. Showing special objects related to an assembly or trip to the child before or after the activity is also an important enrichment experience.

Troubleshooting

Although an aide can provide enrichment during activities like assemblies and school trips, it is very important that the blind/VI student sit with classmates and interact with them, not just with the aide. As the blind/VI student gets older, classmates naturally take over these activities. Teachers should keep a discreet watch over this process to make sure it does not become a burden to the other students. Teachers should also identify ways in which the blind/VI student can reciprocate by providing a service for others. Avoid an environment in which the blind/VI student is always the receiver and never the giver of assistance.

THE IMPORTANCE OF GOOD JUDGMENT

An aide finds him/herself making decisions every few minutes throughout the day. Should I intervene in this situation or not? We're running out of time, should I do this for the student this one time? Would this be a good time to interrupt the teacher? Should I run into the classroom and give the child this information right now or would it be better to wait? When can I find some time to fit in these extras I've been saving to show the student?

A good understanding of the functioning of the classroom and of the teacher's routine and priorities will help you make these difficult decisions. Another aid to decision making is gauging each decision against the goal of independence. Will what I am about to do move this student toward independence? *Make sure that your decisions over the course of time are helping the child to progress toward independence.* Don't fall into the habit of assisting too much. Develop a good feel for when to step in and when to step back.

Another useful exercise is to think about the consequences of your decisions and actions. How will what I am about to do affect this child? Will it teach him/her a skill? Will it make him/her more competent? What unspoken messages will it send?

WATCH FOR THESE COMMON DANGER AREAS!

Having an aide in the classroom can be a great help to both student and classroom teacher, but watch for these common danger areas—learned dependence, a class within a class, special relationships, and acting on assumptions of help needed.

Learned Dependence

The most common pitfall of having an aide in the classroom is learned dependence. Instead of learning more about *independence* each day, the blind/VI child learns more about *dependence*. It is easy to assist too much—to open the book for the child, to find the page, to accompany the child from place to place. The appropriate role for the aide is to *teach* opening the book, to *give the child practice* in finding the page quickly, and to *encourage independent movement* throughout the classroom and school. If the aide gives too much help, the child will not learn to do the tasks and will not develop an inner expectation that he/she is capable of doing them and should be doing them.

Don't hover. Don't overprotect. Keep a watchful eye, but don't step in unless it's necessary. Use good judgment. Base your interventions on the idea of an independent future for the child, not on the idea that blind/VI people cannot be expected to do certain tasks.

A Class Within a Class

Another pitfall to avoid is letting a private conversation develop in the classroom, with the aide and the blind/VI student becoming a separate class in the back of the room. The teacher teaches the class; the aide teaches the blind/VI child. Occasionally this might be appropriate, for example, if the blind/VI student is using completely different materials from those of sighted classmates, *but the goal is always for the child to be a full participant in class, paying attention to and being taught by the teacher.*

The child needs to learn to focus on the teacher, pay attention to the instructions, translate them if necessary into what would make sense for braille or other adaptations, and then get going! Likewise, the teacher should not use the aide as an intermediary, but should speak directly to the student.

The aide might enjoy the private conversation; the child might enjoy it; even the teacher might desire it. But it won't get the child where the child needs to go.

Special Relationships

A related danger area is that of special relationships. Blind/VI children can develop extremely close bonds with the people—almost always adults—who work with them one-to-one. These are often warm, loving relationships, but they can interrupt the process toward independence.

For example, a special relationship can keep a child from mastering a task. From the time Claudia, a blind/VI student, was in kindergarten, a sixth grade big sister walked her down the long hill outside their school. Each year a wonderful relationship developed between Claudia and the older girl, *but Claudia never learned her way down the hill!* Claudia's parents finally realized—at the beginning of third grade—that the girls had to come down the hill without chatting until Claudia learned her way. Claudia did finally learn her way down the hill, but not until the parents intervened.

Special relationships can be a problem in another area. Because they are usually between the blind/VI child and an adult or an older child, these relationships can impede the development of friendships with peers. Everyone in the school gets used to seeing the blind/VI child with the aide. The adults get used to it and, of even greater concern, the other children get used to it. The attitude develops that the blind/VI child belongs to the aide. If the blind/VI child is walking along or looking for other children to join in with, someone returns him or her to the aide, since that is where the blind/VI child belongs. This attitude can even develop within the blind/VI child him/herself. Being with an adult all the time becomes so familiar and comfortable to the blind/VI child that he or she does not develop any self-expectation for normal social interactions with peers.

It is very tempting to let special relationships develop—they come out of the goodness of people's hearts—but they are not, in the long run, in the best interest of the blind/VI child.

Acting on Assumptions of Help Needed

So many times sighted people assume that the blind/VI child cannot do something independently. This assumption is usually based on the idea of the helpless blind/VI person or the idea that eyesight is necessary to accomplish the task. But so often the assumption will not be true—the child can actually do the task. Perhaps you think that the child will be unsafe on the stairs, or lacks the hand strength to use the water fountain, or doesn't have the ability to find the door handle to open the door.

Give the student a chance to try the task. If he/she really cannot perform it, *then make sure someone teaches him/her the skills necessary to do it!* Many times you will discover that the child can indeed do the task. So don't act on assumptions, question them!

STRAIGHT TALK ON SOME TOUCHY SUBJECTS

When there is an aide in the classroom, a few sensitive areas exist that can keep the education of the blind/VI student from going smoothly and could even derail it. If administrators, teachers, and aides give thought to these areas in advance, it can save anguish later.

Attitudes and Emotions

It is important to be matter-of-fact about blindness/visual impairment and the aide's contribution to the student's success. The job of the aide is to level the playing field so that the blind/VI student has equal access to materials and information. The aide's contribution should be appreciated, but in the same way that the contribution of any teacher is appreciated. Try not to let the attitude develop around the school that the aide is the child's—or the teacher's—savior. (This may sound harsh or extreme, but it is common.) Keep the emphasis on how the child is learning skills and becoming independent, not on how wonderful the aide is for helping.

Since the aide's help should be aimed at the child's mastering of skills, as the child makes progress, less help will be necessary. The aide must be prepared for this eventuality. This does not mean the aide's work is not important; it means that his/her work must be aimed at producing a more independent student. The aide should measure his/her own success not by how much the child needs him/her or how important he/she is to the program, but by how independent the child becomes on his/her watch. If the aide has this attitude, then there will be a much better chance of success for the blind/VI student's education.

The work of an aide is important, and it is natural that the aide would want his/her role to be appreciated, respected, and valued. Sometimes, however, the desire of the aide to remain a central part of the blind/VI child's educational process gets in the way of the student's progress toward independence. Don't let the aide's desire to be important trump the student's right to be independent! The aide needs to remember the goal of independence and to keep stepping back. This is not only appropriate but *necessary* for the child's progress. An aide must not take over the process of the child's education, but must allow the child to take the normal and appropriate steps toward autonomy and self-determination. So, when referring to the aide and his/her work, find the middle ground—the aide should never be made to feel unimportant to the process, but neither should he/she feel that the child would be nowhere without him/her.

Sometimes an aide gets too emotionally close to a student. Certainly, a close, loving relationship can be fine and indeed beneficial to the child. But this is another time when a fine line must be walked. The relationship between an aide and a student must be like the relationship between a teacher and a student. There can and should be bonding, warmth, closeness, even love. But just as the teacher and the students can manage to move on at the end of the year, so must the aide and the blind/VI student be able to move on to the next step toward independence.

Is the Aide an Expert on Blindness?

The longer an aide works with a blind/VI student, the more the temptation to look upon the aide as an expert on blindness/visual impairment. But chances are his/her experience with blindness/visual impairment is not extensive; the blind/VI student he/she is working with may well be the first blind/VI person the aide has ever gotten to know. There is a danger in teachers' turning to the aide for advice and information about presenting concepts to the blind/VI student, testing adaptations, use of the cane, any number of things. The aide might have very good instincts and have much to offer in this area, but most of the time it is in the best interest of the student to consult with the TVI, competent blind/VI adults, the parents, especially if they are active in an organization such as the National Federation of the Blind (see Resources, page 207), or, most important, the student him/herself.

Again, a fine line must be walked between respecting the knowledge the aide has gained on the job through his/her interaction with the student and the TVI, and realizing that he/she is still probably not well versed in blindness/visual impairment issues. It is natural to want to be asked for information and an aide may have hurt feelings if he/she is not consulted; after all, he/she does get to know the child. However, the fact remains that he/she is probably not an expert on blindness/visual impairment.

The aide must agree that as the student gets older and gains competence, *the student* must become the expert on blindness/visual impairment and its tools and techniques. If the team has done its job, the student will have been exposed to the tools and methods that exist and encouraged to determine which method works best for the task. The student will then be ready and able to take on the decision making regarding these issues.

The caveats are the same for a technical assistant (please see page 144). The technical assistant should not be viewed as an expert on blindness/visual impairment; teachers should still confer with the student, parents, and TVI on blindness/visual impairment issues. The technical assistant should not make curriculum decisions; those belong to the teacher and the IEP team.

The Classroom Teacher Is Not Ready for the Aide to Leave

You may face the situation in which the classroom teacher does not want the aide to leave the room, even though the student is ready to participate in class on his or her own. Perhaps the teacher could be put in touch with some competent blind/VI adults who could explain or demonstrate some of the independent living techniques they use and help the teacher envision an independent future for the student. In any case, the student's need for independence must come before the teacher's fears.

Talking in Front of the Student

A common phenomenon is for the classroom teacher and aide to discuss the student within the student's earshot. Listening can be very highly developed in the young blind/VI child, so be sure to observe the common courtesies in this area.

What Is *Not* the Role of the Aide?

In addition to the many duties an aide might be responsible for, there are others that would be inappropriate and should be avoided. The student's progress in several areas—independent classroom functioning, interaction with the teacher, independent movement, social interaction—is at stake. Some roles that the aide should *not* take on are the following:

- *Decision maker about curriculum.*   Any decisions about curriculum and material the student will be responsible for must be made by the teacher and the IEP team.
- *Grader of papers.*   Unless the teacher asks the aide to grade the papers of all the students in the class, the aide should not be correcting or grading the blind/VI student's papers. The teacher must be the one to do it. Likewise, the aide should not reprimand the student if work is not complete or done satisfactorily; that is the teacher's job.
- *Private teacher/tutor.*   The student must learn to pay attention to the teacher, follow directions, and get to work.

- *Decision maker about blindness/visual impairment techniques.* Unless the aide is a skilled blind/VI person him/herself, the aide is probably not the person to make decisions about what techniques the blind/VI student should be using for various tasks.

- *Decision maker about cane use.* Decisions about cane use should be made by the student, parents, and O&M instructor. It is rare that anyone should ever tell the blind/VI student *not* to use the cane in a certain area or situation if the child prefers to use it.

- *Sighted guide.* The student should be moving about independently and learning to be responsible for his/her own movement. The sighted guide technique should be used sparingly, at most. If it is used, the student should still use his/her cane.

- *Playmate.* For the youngest child, the aide often serves as a facilitator of social interaction and play. But he/she should be helping the child learn to play with other children. If the aide is the child's constant companion on the playground, social interaction will be impeded.

- *Protector on the playground.* The process of teaching the student playground safety skills should begin in preschool, so that the child can be as safe and independent in play as the other children. The protection can only be removed if the child learns the skills, so make sure they are being taught!

- *Overseer.* The child should be learning skills and making progress toward independence. As skills develop, supervision and guidance should lessen. The student should be encouraged to make the normal, appropriate moves toward independence and self-sufficiency.

- *Guardian in the hallways.* Again, as the student gets older and gains skill, he/she must be allowed the same level of independent mobility as sighted peers.

SCHOOL ADMINISTRATORS MUST BE ON BOARD

It is critically important for school administrators and the IEP team to understand the overriding goal of independence. To achieve this goal, the balance must shift from more help from adults to less help, from dependence to independence. With the input and approval of administrators, a plan should be put in place for the gradual and sensible lessening of the time the aide spends with the blind/VI student. Without a written plan, independence may never be achieved! If the school principal is conscious of the blind/VI student's need to move toward independence, then he/she will not inadvertently edge the child toward learned dependence by insisting that the aide be at the child's side at all times.

The goal of independence means there will be times that the aide is giving no assistance at all to the blind/VI student. These moments should become more and more frequent as time goes on. At all times when the blind/VI student is able to work unassisted, *the aide must feel free to do nothing.* If the aide feels that he/she will be criticized or penalized for doing nothing he/she will be more likely to hover and be with the student even when the student does not need help. This will impede the process of independence. If administrators occasionally reinforce the necessity of gradually diminishing the aide's direct involvement with the student, the aide will feel free to step back.

How is the aide referred to at your school? Is he/she considered a personal aide to the child or an aide to the teacher? If the aide is referred to as the child's aide, then there's a good chance that the blind/VI child and his/her classmates will perceive the blind/VI child as helpless or in need of constant protection or supervision. Using another term such as teacher's aide, classroom aide, or paraprofessional can help prevent this problem. As always, think of the future—the child must be encouraged in normal steps toward independence and responsibility for him/herself.

AN INDEPENDENCE PLAN

Here is what an independence plan might look like: The blind/VI student is doing very well in music class and almost never needs assistance from the aide in that class. So music could become the first class in which the child will participate without the aide. If teachers are a little shaky about the idea, the aide could spend the class period nearby for the first few times and be on call, so to speak, in case he/she is needed. After a few classes, when everyone is feeling more secure, the aide could spend the class period consulting with the classroom teacher or adapting materials.

What might be the next independence goal? Perhaps the student is unable to walk in line independently and get to the class without assistance from the aide. If so, then learning the way to the class and/or learning to walk in line with classmates could be the next independence focus.

The team could then begin looking at the next logical place for the child to participate independently. Perhaps it might be reading time or social studies period. In this way, little by little, the student will learn to function on an independent basis at school. As the shift toward independent participation occurs, there will also be a shift in the aide's duties, more and more toward background work—creating adapted illustrations and models, producing braille or large print, and so forth.

THE TRANSITION TO TECHNICAL ASSISTANT

When the time comes that the aide is only rarely needed in the classroom, plan for him/her to become a technical assistant. The main difference between an aide and a technical assistant is that the technical assistant does not provide direct assistance to the student. Instead, he/she concentrates on the background work—creating braille or enlarging pages, adapting illustrations, keeping track of special equipment and materials, and so forth. Occasionally he/she will serve as a reader. (A reader is someone who reads print material aloud for a blind/VI person. See Using Readers, page 35, for a full discussion of this skill.)

As the reading demands grow heavier and more varied in the higher grades, braille transcribing needs increase. Depending on the school's curriculum and the amount of material that needs to be put into an alternative medium, the technical assistant position might be full or part time. It might make sense for him/her to spend some of his/her free time assisting in another room. (Make sure the parents understand that this reflects their child's progress toward independence, so that they will not fear that the school is taking away the aide just to save money!)

The aide who is transitioning into the position of technical assistant may very well miss the daily interaction with the child and may feel lonely. This problem is compounded if the new work area is off in an isolated area of the school, away from other school personnel. If possible, place the new workstation in an area where the technical assistant can be in contact with other school staff. This usually works out fine until the technical assistant needs to turn on the braille embosser—it's loud! In order to avoid disturbing others, the technical assistant can schedule embossing for times when no one else is present.

The work area needs to be large enough to house the equipment and materials the technical assistant will use, such as a computer, an embosser, a work table, and so forth; if a large enough space is available, it could also be used to store the student's special equipment, books, and so forth.

BRINGING THE DAY OF INDEPENDENCE CLOSER

Remember that the goal is to keep the student progressing toward independence. As time passes, the balance must shift from more individual help and less independence in the early years to less individual help and more independence as the child grows older and gains skill. We want the student to be able to manage on his/her own, not always to require a high level of assistance from us.

The adults in the child's life must make sure the child learns all the skills necessary for independence. Then we must keep stepping back. Each new skill the child learns, each activity he or she is able to take over, brings the day of independence closer. The bottom line is, we've got to work ourselves out of a job!

CHAPTER 10

ADAPTING MATERIALS

One of the keys to making the education of a blind/visually impaired student work is to have materials in a form accessible to the student and to have those accessible materials ready at the time they are needed in class. In addition to books and other written matter in braille or enlarged form, accessible materials could include real items, models, manipulatives, tactile illustrations, auditory information, and so forth.

Textbooks needed in braille or large print are usually provided by the agency or entity serving blind/VI students in your state or region. Ancillary materials, however, may not be provided. School districts often report difficulty in getting workbooks, practice materials, and sometimes tests in adapted form.

Schools sometimes have a staff member on board whose job it is to create materials in braille, enlarged form, or tactile form for the student. This could be a classroom aide or an aide who no longer works directly with the student and has transitioned into a technical assistant position (see page 144).

A PLAN FOR GETTING MATERIALS ADAPTED

The classroom teacher and technical assistant must create a system for getting materials adapted in a timely manner so that materials are ready for class when they are needed. As the technical assistant gains experience in adapting items, he/she will be able to estimate how much lead time is

Making It Work: Educating the Blind/VI Student in the Regular School, 147–160
Copyright © 2005 by Information Age Publishing

required in order to get things back to the teacher by the date needed. Following are some tips:

- Plan and discuss adapting needs *in advance* so that the technical assistant has enough time to create the materials.
- Designate a place to drop off and pick up materials.
- Mark all materials to be adapted with the date needed for class.
- The technical assistant can look through braille textbooks to determine if maps, diagrams, and so forth have been omitted. The teacher can then decide which of the omitted items will actually be needed and give the technical assistant due dates.
- If any adjustments to the content, goals, and material that the student will be responsible for are necessary due to a learning disability, the teacher should first make those determinations and then see which material needs to be adapted for blindness/visual impairment. The technical assistant creates the accessible materials; all decisions about content must remain the responsibility of the teacher.
- Build in some regular meeting time to plan, share adaptation ideas, and discuss how adaptations have been working. Ask the student for feedback.
- 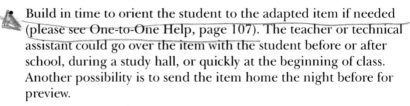 Build in time to orient the student to the adapted item if needed (please see One-to-One Help, page 107). The teacher or technical assistant could go over the item with the student before or after school, during a study hall, or quickly at the beginning of class. Another possibility is to send the item home the night before for preview.

Enlarging Print Materials

- Find out what type size works best for your student.
- Use a clear san serif font like Arial bold or Helvetica.
- The 155% setting on a photocopier enlarges standard print to about 20 point type and fits on an 11 × 17 sheet of paper.
- Also provide the student with the material in its original size, in case something gets cut off in the enlarging process.

Enlarging Illustrations

- Work with your student to determine how large to make illustrations. If an illustration is particularly complex, consider adding color to certain areas to distinguish them from other nearby areas.

- Make sure captions stay with their illustrations.
- Be very careful when enlarging maps to make sure that the map key is enlarged to the same percentage as the map itself. If they are at different percentages, all the student's calculations of distance will be wrong!
- The same holds true for any diagrams in math or science involving measurement. If the diagram is enlarged, the measuring-unit drawing must also be enlarged, and to the same percentage.
- If the assignment entails using a real ruler, the student may want to work with the original size diagram, using a magnifier or CCTV. Another option is to photocopy and enlarge the real ruler to the same percentage as the enlarged diagram.

Creating Braille from Print Materials

Braille can be written manually on a braillewriting machine. Most technical assistants, however, create braille using a computer and braille embosser setup. The material to be brailled can either be typed or scanned into the computer.

For *typing in* the material, the components needed are the following:

- braille translation software
- braille embosser (often referred to as a braille printer)

For *scanning in* the material, the components needed are as follows:

- scanner
- optical character recognition (OCR) software
- braille translation software
- braille embosser

Inputting the Material

Here are the general steps for typing or scanning the document into the computer:

- Type the material directly into a new document in the braille translation program; or type the material into a word processing program and then open it with the braille translation program or cut-and-paste it into the braille translation program.
- The other option is to scan the print document and run it through the OCR software. The OCR turns the scan from an image of a

print page into a document that can be manipulated. Open the document with the braille translation program or cut-and-paste it in.

Translating from Print to Braille

The basic steps for translating the document from print into braille are as follows:

- With the document open on the screen in the braille translation program, fine-tune the format (see Troubleshooting, below), spell check, and proofread.
- Use the translate command in the braille translation program. The braille version can then be viewed on the screen, along with a corresponding line of print in a frame at the bottom of the screen. Double-check and fine-tune the formatting.
- Send the document to the braille embosser.

The Braille Document

With a little basic knowledge of braille and by keeping track of the way the braille paper comes out of the embosser, the technical assistant will be able to figure out which is the top of the page.

- Write in the first few words in print at the top of the first braille page to identify the document.
- Pull the sheets apart, keeping them in order.
- Place the print original on top and staple the pages together.
- Place the document in the designated spot for the classroom teacher.

Troubleshooting

Some fine-tuning of the document format before brailling is almost always required so that the braille document will be usable. Some examples are as follows:

- If parts of the original print document are laid out in columns, those columns will probably have to be reformatted as lists. Do this step either in the word processing program or while the print is still on the screen in the braille translation program (before giving the command to translate into braille). Here is an example.

Print original:

5. A simple machine that has a fulcrum is called a
    A. pulley   C. inclined plane
    B. lever   D. wedge

Braille format:

5. A simple machine that has a fulcrum is called a
    A. pulley
    B. lever
    C. inclined plane
    D. wedge

- Check to see that paragraphs are indented and get rid of extra space. Do this step in the translation program when the braille version is on the screen.
- Keep the various parts of a question together, if possible, especially for young students. Examples are a multipart question or a question and its multiple choice answers. It's often better to push the whole question onto a new page rather than separate it over two pages. Do this step when the braille is on the screen.
- Math in braille has special characters and requires exact spacing. Programs do exist for inputting mathematics via the computer, but these are best left to trained braille transcribers. Usually the TVI handles the extra math papers that need to be done the good old-fashioned way—on the braillewriter. Math must be left to the experts!
- World languages can be brailled via the computer. Many languages are written in uncontracted (Grade 1) braille except for accented letters which require special braille signs. Check with your TVI for details for your student's world language.
- Test out the braille created on the computer, especially at first, with the blind/VI student. The student can give feedback on how the formatting is working and offer useful suggestions.

TACTILE ILLUSTRATIONS

Young blind/VI students need a great deal of hands-on experience with objects so that they can form a proper understanding of the world. For the youngest blind/VI students, therefore, the first tactile illustrations should consist of real items, whenever possible. For example, if the lesson is on categorizing and the sighted children are looking at pictures of fruit, give the blind/VI student real fruit to handle instead of wooden or plastic models or raised-line drawings. After enough experiences with the real thing, the child will be ready to recognize that the model is made to look in certain ways like the real object. (For example, size and shape might be the same, but texture, weight, temperature may be very different!)

In other situations, again with the very young student, a model will not be of much use at all. For example, if the lesson is about animals, showing a very young child a model of a cow will not teach the child what a cow is like and may indeed give the child a set of incorrect ideas. In a case like this, discuss the upcoming lesson with the TVI and the family. Perhaps some kind of real experience, such as a trip to a farm, can be arranged. After the child has had experience with the real thing, a model might be useful.

In math class in the early grades, it is important to provide the blind/VI student with effective manipulatives so that basic arithmetic concepts can be internalized. (Effective manipulatives would be color- and texture-coded and could be attached to each other, a backing or form, or a magnet board so that the child can easily keep track of them. Also provide a box or tray with edges so the items will not fall off the desk.) Although raised-line drawings will probably be in the student's math textbook (unlike other textbooks), the student in the early grades will probably benefit more from using hands-on items rather than the drawings—or hands-on items in addition to the drawings. In fact, putting something in the student's hands often solves what might look like a learning difficulty. As with all children, concrete experiences must precede more abstract representations.

After adequate experience with real objects and three-dimensional models, the young blind/VI child will be ready to begin learning from two-dimensional illustrations (see Interpreting Tactile Graphics, page 34).

What Makes a Good Tactile Illustration?

Many textbooks rely on photos, drawings, and diagrams to illustrate concepts being presented. Illustrations such as maps, charts, and diagrams, however, are usually omitted from the braille version of textbooks, leaving the blind/VI student without these learning aids. (In recorded textbooks the narrator describes illustrations, but the student might still benefit from a good, clear accessible illustration.)

There are some differences in how pictorial material is taken in through the eyes and through the fingers. For example, the eye glances at the whole and then begins to perceive details, while the fingers use details to piece together the whole. Because of differences like this, the idea when creating a tactile illustration is not always simply to duplicate exactly the print illustration in tactile form. This could produce a confusing, overly complex result. Here are some guidelines to follow in order to make usable illustrations for a blind/VI student.

- Think about whether you should attempt to make a drawing or find a 3-D model. In many instances, especially for the youngest students, a model is a more effective learning tool. Of course, use the real thing whenever possible.

- Analyze the purpose of the print illustration to make sure the adapted illustration communicates the intended message. Meet with the teacher when necessary to determine the point of the lesson and plan the adaptation.

- Size the illustration properly. It needs to be large enough so that there is space between lines, but small enough that it can be understood as a whole.

- Keep the illustration simple, clear, and uncluttered. For the sake of clarity, omit details that are not necessary, even if they are in the print original. Remember, it is the concept that must come across.

- Sometimes, however, it is critical to follow the print original exactly, for example, if the lesson is on measuring angles or learning about scale.

- Keep lines on graphics at least one-eighth of an inch apart. Lines closer together than this cannot be discerned.

- When deciding on tactile materials, choose firm materials that will enable the student to feel edges. Self-stick cork will work; self-stick felt probably won't.

- Choose *low* materials that enable the student to feel both the shape and the background at the same time. This gives the student more information and makes the illustration more effective, by enabling the student to perceive the relationship of the raised area to its background or context.

- Cardboard and string can become your best friends. Thin cardboard that is easy to cut is an excellent material for tactile illustrations. String cut to the right length and glued down makes a very good line. Both cardboard and string are *low* and allow the student to see the shape and the background at the same time.

- Add labels in braille when needed.

- When needed, use a key to tell the student what the various textures signify.
- Close your eyes and test your tactile illustration with your own fingers. If you can't make sense of it, your student probably won't be able to, either.
- If your illustration is visually beautiful, watch out! It may not work at all when read with the fingers. In addition, some textures that are pleasing visually, such as glitter, feel rough and scratchy to the fingers.
- Get feedback on your illustrations from the student. You need to know whether what you are making is actually working for the student.
- Don't have hurt feelings if a drawing does not work! Experiment with different materials until you find the right ones for the job.
- Consult with the TVI and the child's family. They have probably had a great deal of experience with tactile materials.
- A great deal of information is available if you want to learn more about making tactile graphics. Check Resources, page 194, for several sources; also, a computer search for tactile graphics will turn up a wealth of information.

Materials to Have in Your Bag of Tricks

Many items useful for making tactile illustrations are available at regular stores or from catalogs of items made especially for blind/VI people. A list of materials follows. Peruse the shelves of the nearest craft store for more ideas. The Resources chapter, page 187, gives sources for the special items.

- Cardboard: Start saving the cardboard from pads of paper. It's a good thickness to use—thin enough to cut easily and to let the student perceive the shape and the background at the same time.
- String: Cut the string to the right length. Apply the glue to the paper or cardboard. Place the string down.
- Glue: Useful for attaching shapes, but can also be used to make a raised-line outline. Make sure you build in enough time for the glue to dry.
- Double-sided tape: An alternative to glue.
- Wikki Stix: A craft/art item made of waxed string. Great for raised-line drawings and outlining shapes.
- Self-stick textures: Intended for use on the bottom of lamps, bookends, and so forth, to keep them from scratching the furniture,

these little pieces of cork, foam, plastic dome, and so on, can be used to adapt worksheets, make graphs, and so forth.

- Velcro: Intended as a fastener, self-stick Velcro can be used to adapt materials as above.

- Wooden craft pieces: Wooden shapes from the craft store are useful for adapting worksheets and making pictures.

- Braille labeler and tape: Produces braille on self-stick plastic tape. Dial has both print and braille letters for easy use. Useful for labeling tactile illustrations, but be aware that only the most commonly occurring braille contractions are included on the dial. Clear tape is handiest.

- Laminating sheets: Clear plastic sheets with self-stick backing can be rolled into the braillewriter. Useful for labeling tactile illustrations when more braille needs to be written than would fit on labeling tape.

- Coloring screen: Cut a piece of window screening and a piece of sturdy cardboard 9 × 12 or larger. Place the screening over the cardboard and secure the edges with duct or gaffer's tape, covering all edges of the screening. Place a piece of regular paper over the screen and draw with a crayon or ballpoint pen for an instant raised-line drawing.

- Tactile Marking Mat: Instead of making a coloring screen, you can purchase a tactile marking mat. Place a piece of regular paper over this bumpy plastic sheet and draw with a crayon for an instant raised-line drawing.

- Sewell Raised Line Drawing Kit: A special tool made for blind/VI people, this kit contains a clipboard, plastic sheets, and a stylus.

- Tracing wheel: Intended as a sewing tool, a tracing wheel can be used to make raised-line drawings. Place print original wrong side up over a rubber pad or pile of newspapers. Trace along the outlines with the tracing wheel. A feelable line will result on the other side. If a sturdier drawing is needed, first trace the print original onto braille paper and then go over it with the tracing wheel.

- Swail Dot Inverter: A special tool made for blind/VI people. Place braille paper over a rubber pad. Press the dot inverter stylus. Individual raised dots result. Useful for tactile drawings, charts, graphs, and so forth.

- Tactile image makers: Thermal machines for creating raised-line pictures from print originals (see Resources, page 194). Make a copy of the picture onto special heat-sensitive paper in a copy machine. Run the copy through the thermal machine for an instant raised-line drawing. Use this tool with caution—resulting pictures are not always usable by the blind/VI student!

- Thermal pen: A heat pen that can make a raised-line drawing when used on special paper.
- Tiger printer: A very high-end braille embosser that can make high-quality tactile graphics from any computer image.

Three Ideas for Tactile Maps

The ability to use a map is a very useful skill to have. Following are ideas for making three different kinds of maps.

Tactile Floor Plan

It is very helpful for a blind/VI student to have a tactile map (Figure 10.1) of the school building, especially when he/she begins to change classes. Following is an easy way to create a tactile floor plan:

- Get a print copy of the floor plan of the building.
- Enlarge or shrink the page in a copy machine to a size where the hallways would be about three-eighths of an inch wide.
- Use a piece of foam posterboard as a backing. Cut it to the size you need.
- Place the sized page over thin cardboard. Trace over the lines of the hallways, pressing hard so that the indentations will be visible on the cardboard.
- On this tactile map, the hallways will be white space and the classrooms will be solid cardboard. Cut along the lines you traced using scissors or an X-ACTO knife.
- Use an X-ACTO knife to notch doorways into the cardboard pieces.
- Glue down the cardboard pieces, leaving the three-eighths of an inch spaces as the hallways.
- Glue down pieces of string to indicate steps.
- Experiment with adding braille labels to the map. Make sure the student is looking at the map itself and not just reading the labels.

Map of a Country

Students examine maps of various countries in social studies classes and when they study world languages. Here is a simple way to make a tactile map of a country (see Figure 10.2).

Figure 10.1.   Tactile floor plan.

- Get a print copy of the map of a country and enlarge or shrink it to a good size.
- Place the sheet over thin cardboard. Trace over the outline of the country, pressing hard so that the indentations will be visible on the cardboard.
- Cut along the outline so that you have a piece of cardboard in the shape of the country.
- Customize the map as needed. For example, make internal boundaries by gluing down string; make rivers out of Wikki Stix; use a number of self-stick cork triangles to indicate mountains; a self-stick plastic dome could mark the capital city.

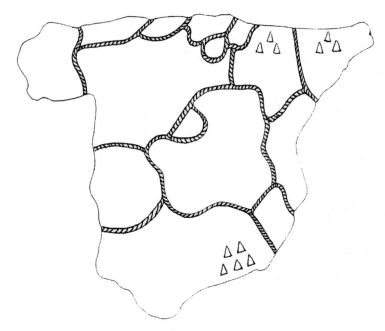

Figure 10.2.   Map of a country.

- You can add braille labels and a map key showing what each texture indicates.

Jigsaw Puzzle Map

A third way to make a map is jigsaw puzzle style (see Figure 10.3). This style works well for maps of areas which include several countries, such as Europe or South America.

- Get a print copy of the map of a country and enlarge or shrink it to a good size.
- Place the sheet over a piece of corrugated cardboard. Trace over the outline and the country boundary lines, pressing hard so that the indentations will be visible on the cardboard.
- Use an X-ACTO knife to cut along the outline, leaving the outer part of the cardboard intact. This piece serves as the form for the country pieces. Glue this piece onto a piece of foamboard.
- Cut the countries apart. If desired, you can use a piece of foam instead of the cardboard to make softer country pieces. Foam pieces have some flexibility and might be easier for your student to handle when pressing the pieces into the form.

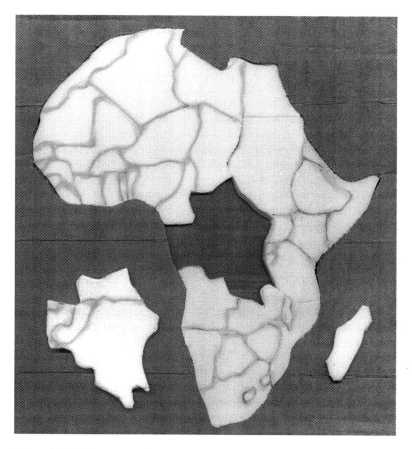

Figure 10.3. Jigzaw puzzle map.

- Add braille labels or a label key, if needed.
- The student can examine the shape of the continent and of each country and then fit the countries together inside the form. If you add braille labels, make sure the student is looking at the map and not just reading the words!

OTHER CONCEPT PRESENTATION IDEAS

Diagrams in science and other textbooks often provide a pictorial display of complex concepts and processes. Usually extremely complicated diagrams do not translate well into tactile form. Following are two alternatives to tactile illustrations that can help get the idea across.

Auditory Diagrams

One alternative to a tactile illustration for getting across very complicated information is an auditory diagram. The science (or other subject) teacher records a description of the process being illustrated in a diagram onto a tape for the student to listen to. Be sure to record the title and figure number of the illustration and to label the tape.

Word Pictures

Blind/VI students at the elementary level use word pictures as an alternative to drawing. Word pictures can also be used in the same way as auditory diagrams, above, as an alternative to complex information presented in pictorial form. Instead of recording the material, the teacher can put it in written form for the student to learn and study from.

Alternative Testing

The student who is learning using some alternative to print illustrations, such as a puzzle map, an auditory diagram, or a word picture, must be tested in a similar alternative fashion. The testing mode must enable him/her to demonstrate understanding of the material. For example, if the class has to label a blank diagram of a scientific process, the blind/VI student might be asked to list all the components of the process in order, based on the information provided in the auditory diagram. If the class must fill in a blank map, the blind/VI student might be asked to name the countries while moving his/her hands across the tactile map (with braille labels removed). Remember to teach, give practice, and test on the same materials.

CHAPTER 11

TECHNOLOGY

Professor Austin reminds her students at the end of sociology class to check the syllabus on the Website for next week's assignment and then hands out a packet of articles. She mentions that the research paper notes are due on Tuesday and adds that she's willing to give some extra credit to students who attend and take notes on the lecture on social justice that evening in the college chapel.

Claudia, a blind student, leaves class and heads back to her dorm. In her room, she uses her speech-equipped computer to quickly check her email and then logs on to the college Website to take a look at the assignment. It sounds interesting—case studies on inner city poverty and values. She follows the link to the Website, begins reading, and then decides she'd rather read this one later. She saves the online article into her document folder, then sends it to her notetaker, where she will read it later in braille.

Claudia decides to take care of the notecards next, before she goes to lunch. She cables her notetaker into her braille printer, and outputs the notes for herself in braille. Then she switches the switchbox and prints them out in print for her professor. She labels the first print sheet in braille with her slate and stylus, then clips the sheets together. She's just about to head out to the dining hall when she remembers the packet. She removes the staple from the wad of pages and places the sheets into the auto doc feeder of her scanner. One by one, the sheets are scanned and recognized by the OCR software on her computer. Claudia names and saves the file and finally goes to lunch.

After a long afternoon of reading and studying, the telephone rings. It's Justin, that nice guy from sociology class. "Were you thinking of going to

Making It Work: Educating the Blind/VI Student in the Regular School, 161–166

that social justice lecture tonight? Great! I'll stop by your room and pick you up. Seven-fifteen sound good?"

Claudia smiles. College may be a lot of hard work, but it has its perks, too. At ten after seven there's a knock on the door. Claudia slips her notetaker over her shoulder and grabs her cane. She's glad she has some extra cafe cash left on her student ID card, in case she and Justin are hungry after the lecture. Ah, she thinks, life is sweet.

Can you picture your student doing this someday? He or she is probably not using all of this technology yet, but make sure your student is learning to use the equipment appropriate to his or her level in school or stage of development (see The Skills and Tools of Blindness, page 42).

WHAT TECHNOLOGY DOES MY STUDENT NEED?

Your student's TVI will probably be able to direct the IEP team to an adaptive technology specialist who can evaluate your student' s needs and recommend technology. Technology enables the blind/visually impaired student to easily create and edit documents, produce print and braille hard copy, email and instant message friends, and do online research, just as sighted peers do.

There are a few caveats to heed. First, technology does not replace literacy. Your student still needs to know how to read, write, spell, punctuate, and so forth. Next, technology does not magically fix problems. If your student is having difficulties in school, a new piece of equipment will probably not make the problem disappear. Also, since things change so quickly in the technology world, products that enable nonvisual access to the computer screen are always playing catch-up with the latest innovations for the general public. Lastly, the equipment can be complicated. Make sure your student gets training in the use of the technology, so that it will not end up gathering dust in a corner.

These caveats do not mean that technology is not a valuable or useful investment. It most certainly is! The blind/VI student needs access to the world of technology just as the sighted student does.

Following is an overview of high-tech devices that blind/VI people can make use of. In view of the speed with which technology changes, this section describes categories of equipment, rather than specific devices. Many sources of information are also available on the Internet. The Technology Resource List at www.nfb.org/tech/computer.htm is a good place to start. The International Braille and Technology Center for the Blind in Baltimore will consult free of charge over the telephone. Call 410-659-9314.

COMPUTER ACCESS

Blind/VI students can access computers via screen enlargement, speech, or braille.

- Special screen enlargement software can enlarge to a higher degree than the accessibility features included in the operating system of the computer.
- Screen enlargement can be used in conjunction with speech.
- Speech access programs read what is on the screen. Earphones can be connected for quiet use.
- Speech can be set to announce keystrokes, so that the student can hear each letter as he/she types.
- A refreshable braille display shows what is on the screen via a line of braille cells.
- Students who cannot see the screen use keyboard commands instead of the mouse to navigate around the screen.

ELECTRONIC NOTETAKERS

Notetakers are small, lightweight, portable computer devices. Made specifically for blind/VI people, these screenless talking devices can be used for word processing, checking email, and a variety of other tasks. Students bring them to class and take notes on them; notes can be saved in files and folders. Notetakers take the place of a paper notebook.

- Notetakers can have either a braille or a QWERTY keyboard.
- In addition to speech, notetakers can have a braille display.
- Notetakers include a calendar, datebook, address book, clock, timer, and scientific calculator, among other features.
- Language modules complete with accent marks and spellcheck can be added.
- These handy devices can even be equipped with a global positioning system (GPS).
- A notetaker can be synched to a PC to exchange files.
- Files can be downloaded from a computer or the Internet onto the notetaker to be read via braille or speech.
- A notetaker can connect to a printer or braille embosser to produce print and braille hard copies of documents. When choosing a notetaker, be sure to find out which printers it is compatible with.

BRAILLE EMBOSSERS

Braille embossers—commonly referred to as braille printers—can be connected to a computer or notetaker to produce a braille hard copy of a document. Braille translation software is needed to run a braille embosser from a computer.

- Material can be typed or scanned into the computer, translated into braille via the braille translation software, and then sent to the braille embosser. (Please also see Adapting Materials, page 149.)
- A computer station at school can be set up with a switchbox leading from the computer to both a printer and a braille embosser. Teachers can create a document on the computer, send it to the printer, and then translate it into braille and send it to the braille embosser, too, thus producing copies for both the blind and sighted students in the class.

SCAN-AND-READ SYSTEMS

Scan-and-read systems use a scanner and optical character recognition software (OCR) to scan a document into the computer and turn it into a file that can be read on the screen, listened to, edited, brailled, or sent to a notetaker.

ELECTRONIC BOOKS

Books in electronic form are available from an ever-growing number of sources, both general and specialized for blind/VI readers. Within the specialized sources, leisure reading books are available from the National Library Service for the Blind and Physically Handicapped (NLS) and National Braille Press; Bookshare.org offers a wide variety of books which have been scanned in by members and volunteers; electronic versions of textbooks for students with disabilities can be obtained directly from the publishers.

- NLS operates a free lending library of books for blind/VI users. In addition to books in braille, large print, and recorded form, NLS also provides Web-Braille, braille books on the Internet that can be downloaded into a notetaker.
- Bookshare.org offers downloadable books to be read on a computer via enlargement or speech or on a notetaker via braille or speech; the files can also be embossed into hard copy braille.

- Textbook publishers can provide electronic files free of charge as an accessible alternative to the print book. Electronic files of books can be read on the computer via screen enlargement or speech or can be sent to a notetaker for reading via speech or braille.
  - Publishers might send files on a floppy disk, CD, or even as an email attachment.
  - There is no standard format for these files, so successful users need good computer skills. The younger student would probably need assistance in order to use such e-files.

DIGITAL TALKING BOOKS

In the past, books were recorded on cassette tape. Students using books on tape had to deal with several tapes—sometimes many tapes—per book. A student trying to search a book for a certain section or quotation usually had to spend considerable time in the attempt.

The newer digital recording technology provides several advantages over tapes—books usually fit on one CD; the files are navigable by page, heading, and chapter; the user can bookmark passages and, with computer playback, make notes in the book.

- In addition to books in braille, large print, and Web-Braille, the National Library Service provides leisure reading books on cassette tape and soon will be offering digitally recorded books. These books will require a special playback device.
- The main provider of textbooks in recorded form is Recording for the Blind & Dyslexic (RFB&D). Older books in RFB&D's library were recorded on cassette tape. New books are recorded digitally on CDs. These books require a special playback device or computer program.

CCTV/VIDEO MAGNIFIERS

CCTVs (closed circuit televisions), also called video magnifiers, use a camera to magnify items onto a monitor. Books, papers, illustrations, maps, photos, objects, and so forth, are placed under the camera and then can be viewed in magnified size on the screen. Writing tasks can also be completed under the camera; the user can see what he/she is writing on the screen. CCTVs can be black and white or full color. Some can connect to a computer screen. There are portable and desktop models.

OTHER ITEMS

- The Mountbatten Brailler is a multifunction electronic braille-writer. The student can use it for his/her braille work; a popular feature is that it allows erasing/over-writing of the braille. The student can create and edit files and send them back and forth to a computer. The Mountbatten can be connected to a printer to produce a print copy of what has been brailled. When connected to a keyboard, the Mountbatten can also function as a braille embosser.

- Electronic or interactive whiteboard technology enables the teacher to send information written or displayed on the board at the front of the room to a laptop or PC monitor at the student's desk.

- The Franklin Language Master Special Edition electronic dictionary has a QWERTY keyboard for entering words. The Franklin reads entries out loud, spells words out, and has a thesaurus and word games.

- The IntelliTools system can be adapted for use with blind/VI students (see Resources, page 193).

CHAPTER 12

REPORT FROM THE CLASSROOM

Inspiration and Advice from Those Who Have Been There

THE ONE WHO TAUGHT ME

When I was first informed that I was going to have a blind student in my class, this big, huge question mark loomed over my head—it was a question about myself. Was I going to be able to teach a child who was blind? What do I need to know to teach a child who is blind? How was I going to adapt my lessons so she would get the most out of them? What about written assignments? How would I read what she writes? How would she read what I write? What about the materials she would need? What about the materials I would need? What about the physical aspect of it? Something as simple as her desk. What about the set up of my room—how would she get around? Should I say the word *blind* or *see*?

In all honesty, the only people I ever really knew of who were blind were famous people. I could name them for you—Ray Charles, Stevie Wonder, and I had read about Helen Keller. I had never really met a blind person before, let alone had the opportunity to teach one. I told myself that I needed to approach that teaching year the way I would approach any other. Instead of thinking of S. as a special child, I needed to think of her as just

Making It Work: Educating the Blind/VI Student in the Regular School, 167–185
Copyright © 2005 by Information Age Publishing
167

another child that I would share my year with. I needed to think of her as a child with needs like the rest of the children I encounter and we encounter as educators. All of the children we teach have special needs, every single one of them has a need, one way or another. And as educators, we attend to those needs.

But the questions were still there: how was I going to take the visual aspects of my lessons and turn them into the tactile? What other students could see to obtain information, S. was going to have to touch. Some examples of the techniques we used and things we did were: for a unit on the desert, we brought cacti in. For a unit about the ocean, we took a trip there, collected shells, made shell projects. For a unit on simple machines, we constructed them, experimented with them. For a unit on plants, we grew them. For a unit on fungus, we cultivated our own. Yes, there was a fungus among us. In this case, the students made observations and described them to S. They described the shape of the mold, any increases in size from the day before, if moisture was present and how the samples looked through a microscope. S. then took these observations and wrote her own notes.

I found that having a child like S. in our class enhanced our overall communication skills. We were able to describe things to S. and relate them to things she was familiar with. The communication aspect was really, really important. And you'd be surprised at how descriptive children can get when they describe things like…mold.

Talking to teachers that S. had had in prior years was also a help. They shared tips about techniques they found useful. They shared materials. They were eager to share ideas about organization, how they arranged things in the classroom. Most of all, they gave that reassurance and let me know that it was going to be great.

I developed a good working relationship with the Teacher of the Visually Impaired who was very helpful in getting materials, ordering the braille literature we used, and just for general advice and questions we had. Another important person was the Orientation & Mobility Instructor. I found that communicating my observations related to S.'s mobility helped him and his suggestions and strategies were definitely a help to us. As I became more knowledgeable, I learned that the group effort was going to be the most effective. There was no way I could have done this alone, absolutely not. And if I had gone into it with that mindset, we would not have had as productive a year as we had.

There were many people who played a key role in this experience and developing open pathways of communication with them was also of great importance. I believe the working relationship that I developed with my classroom aide was one of the major components of the experience. She and I had to constantly be open to each other's ideas and suggestions. We had to be flexible in our schedules and our approaches and we both had to understand what the key elements were that we wanted to stress.

We also had to be truthful in evaluating things that we tried to implement. One day, she would say that was a wonderful idea, for something I tried to implement. I'd tell her, that was a great job. And of course on other

days, I'd ask what did you think of that? And I'd get the look, like you'd better go back to the drawing board, buddy.

Our best grader of all was S. S. would let us know if we asked. And sometimes if we didn't. Sometimes we needed to ask nothing at all because we'd
hear, "This is great!"

The other pathway of communication that must be kept open is that
between the home and the school. Obviously nobody knows the child better
than the mother and the father. I have to say that the relationship that we
developed between the home and the school played a definite role in the
success we were able to achieve throughout the entire year.

Our administrators played another major role in enabling us to be very
successful. The constant communication and support of the building principal was of vital importance. Being able to approach the administration
regarding any needs we had was a big help. An example of this was making
it possible for both my aide and myself to attend braille lessons provided by
the Red Cross.

As you can see, what I at first believed was just going to be me ended up
incorporating many, many other people. My network grew and we had a
collaborative effort. I can't stress that enough. Collaboration.

Some of the most important people involved in my experience of teaching a blind student I have not mentioned yet. These are the other students
in the class. They were also a key part of the network. The philosophy is that
a blind kid should be a full participant in class. Not only does the teacher
make a blind student become and feel like a participant, but the other students play a major role as well. I have to say that the other students in my
fourth grade class last year viewed S. as just another student, whether it was
breaking up into reading groups, building model roller coasters, planting
lima beans, learning about the rain forest, or playing kickball out on the
playground, S. was just another student. I think it was my approach of viewing S. as just another student that set the tone for them at first.

S. also went out of her way to teach some of the students and make them
feel like they belonged. So it was a two-way street. She used to let the other
students freely use her brailler and helped them when they did it. In fact,
some of the students became quite good at the brailler. In fact, some of the
students became better than their teacher. I was a slow learner. But I had
our aide, I had the other students, and I had S. to help me.

In my class last year we sat in groups of four or five students. There were
no rows. S. was always part of a group. Our groups changed every two weeks.
Due to the fact that we couldn't easily move S's materials—her bookshelf,
her desk, her brailler—we had a rotating system. We couldn't move S's
things so everybody else moved around her. She was able to sit at a new
group every two weeks. Everybody was able to sit with S. and throughout the
year she was able to sit and share with everybody else.

I feel so very fortunate to have had the opportunity to be a part of S's life.
I can't imagine how my career—and my life—would be without having gone
through this learning experience. If I were asked to give some final words of
advice, they would probably be something like this—keep your expectations

high, not only of the blind student, but of yourself. Academically, don't hold back in any way, shape, or form. Blind students thrive on exposure to new knowledge, just like any other student. The sky's definitely the limit. Don't forget, blind children can achieve academically. They'll probably be able to teach you a thing or two. I know one who taught me.

—Jim Stricchiola
Fourth Grade Teacher

ONE OF THE BEST THINGS

I had the pleasure last school year of having two boys as my students, one in my morning Kindergarten and one in my afternoon Kindergarten. They were twin brothers, one totally blind, one visually impaired. At first when I found out I was going to have the boys in my class, I was quite nervous. I had had mainstreamed kids who were in special education classes, but I had never dealt with anything like visual impairment or blindness. My first feeling was, oh no, how am I going to do this? I'm not an expert. I don't know braille. What will I do? I was totally panicked. One of my thoughts was what if I can't teach them to read? What if I can't teach them to write? What if I can't do my job? It's my responsibility that they move on to the next grade.

I decided to read as much as I could. I learned about the importance of independence, of just being the facilitator, and not hovering over the child. As a parent—I have three children of my own—that was always my philosophy anyway, so I felt comfortable with that, not doing things for them that they can do for themselves.

I believed the boys would learn, but I wanted to make sure that they had a positive year emotionally and socially, too. A big part of what happens in Kindergarten is the social experience and I wanted them both to truly be part of the classroom. D. is a lot more outgoing and he knew how to approach people and speak to them. T. is more reserved and it was going to be a little bit more difficult for him. My goal was for each one of them to become a member of the class one hundred percent without any reservations.

The Teacher of the Visually Impaired was a big support. We knew that it would be best for D. and T. if they learned alongside the other children in the class, so I would give my lesson plans to the Teacher of the Visually Impaired, she would introduce those items in her lesson, then the boys would be able to follow in class.

Adapting lessons and materials was challenging. A lot of our solutions came from things we read and a lot came from common sense—what's the objective of the lesson we're going to teach today? If this is the objective, then how can we meet that objective in a different way? We'd look at the paper and say, what's the point of this? If the point is fine motor, then let's get them doing something that's fine motor.

We had an aide in the room, but we chose to present it as two teachers in our classroom. We didn't call her an aide. Aide implies helping. The kids knew they could go to either of us if they needed something, but my role was primarily the teacher for the children and the aide was there primarily for adapting materials. She was not there to sit next to the blind student helping to do the work. Ninety-nine percent of the work with the child was done by me.

At the beginning we went back and forth—do the boys need an aide, does D. need an aide, do we need an aide in the classroom? I was probably the most afraid that if I didn't have an aide, I wouldn't be able to manage it all. The aide was very good about when to be there and when to step back. She used to say, my job is to eliminate my job. As the year went on, a little at a time, she went into the background. By the end of Kindergarten, her job was basically adapting materials.

One of the questions I had when I was starting the year was how was I going to be able to handle all the extra work. I had two classes, thirty-nine children, thirty-nine sets of parents to be responsible to. The idea of extra work was definitely an issue in my mind. What I found was a lot of the work that you'd call "extra" didn't only apply to D. and T. who happen to have a visual impairment; it applied to all the children. When I was adapting a lesson so that it would accommodate the boys, I realized it would also accommodate the other children and make the lesson better. For example, I write a daily story on a chart in the morning. By reading that story out loud and spelling out the words as I'm writing, I realized that the other kids were getting extra as well, the auditory as well as the visual. There were benefits to all the children in the classroom. So if you're concerned that having a blind student is going to take time away from the other children, I think the opposite is true—it gives to the other children as well.

One of the things I decided to do was have the kids work together, which I tend to do anyway. I tell the kids they have to ask two friends to help them before they ask me. It works really well, especially at the beginning of the year because of course I can't help everyone at once. And it follows that anyone who needed help knew they couldn't just come to the teacher, so it didn't make anyone stand out. There was no need for D. or T. to feel different in any way. They followed the procedure just like everyone else. Of course the guideline for everybody was if you can do it yourself, do it yourself.

The second reason for doing that is that it forces the kids to meet somebody else and to have the language skills to say, "Can you help me?" or "I need help opening my milk." You get help today and the next day you can help them do something. It fostered relationships in the classroom.

Social/emotional development is a big part of Kindergarten. One of the goals we had was for both boys to develop peer relationships that were typical of five- or six-year-old children in the classroom, in the cafeteria, on the playground. The academic part was easy; we probably spent the most time on social skills. The boys were used to a lot of adults from the time they were little—occupational therapist, physical therapist, mobility instructor. Now it was time to focus on their relationships with peers. So we spent a lot of time having them go to peers and forcing them to play. Many times they wanted adult attention, but we had to say, "You've got two friends over there waiting for you" or "Look who's in the block area wanting to play with you."

We had to fight ourselves not to help. We wanted to teach, we wanted to help. But we made ourselves step back, just like we would with any other child. You've got to let them fly at some time. The lesson I learned was that the more you step back and the more confidence you have in the student— whether it be a sighted student or a blind student—the more they can do. Many times during the last marking period of Kindergarten, we saw that when we stepped back, D. was able to do for himself. Then I hoped that I hadn't projected any of my fear onto him!

On the playground, for example. We knew he had playground skills, but when you're out there with twenty kids and everyone's climbing and running, it's another story. Kids aren't always looking; somebody can get hurt. We used verbal cues to all the kids—reminding them to follow all the safety rules, not cut anyone off, to look before they jump, etc.—and it ended up not being a problem at all. D. got involved in a kickball game every day with the other kids. He was the pitcher. When he ran the bases, someone stood on the base and yelled to him. He wanted to join in and he did join in.

The social part was the most difficult, but I felt that if they were going to succeed the following year in first grade, we had to make the social part happen. We wanted the boys to establish real relationships, have their peers not just help them, but be friends. I feel that goal was accomplished. We pushed the boys just about as far as they could go. The other kids for the most part were very nonchalant about the whole thing. They didn't think it was a big deal to have a blind child in their classroom. They didn't even take notice of it after the first two weeks.

Another important thing was braille skills. D. has had braille instruction since he was three. His braille skills were strong and his phonics and reading skills were up there. That enabled him to participate one hundred percent in everything. If we were doing a lesson where kids were going to write in their journals, it was no big deal. He just sat down at the braillewriter and did his invented spelling and wrote his sentences. Later on in the year, the kids would work with a buddy and create little books. I would team D. up with somebody who didn't have such great phonics skills. That child wasn't able to write the words, so he would draw the pictures and D. would write the words on the braillewriter.

Teamwork is important—between students, between the teacher and the aide, and also with the parents, the mobility instructor, the braille teacher, the phys ed teacher, the librarian, the Child Study Team, the building principal. We consulted with each other; nobody knew everything. When we put the different puzzle pieces together, that's when it really worked.

A week or two after I started teaching the boys, I began to look at the experience as an opportunity for me to grow as a teacher and hopefully as a person as well. A little at a time, through teamwork, we figured it out. I've since told many people who have asked me about the experience, that it turned out to be one of the best things I've ever done in my entire life, one of the most positive things and feel-good things. I think I got more out of it than the boys did.

—Virginia Scala
Kindergarten Teacher

WHAT A GIFT

I know the emotions you might be feeling. Eagerness, eagerness to find the secrets that will unlock what you might think is the mystery of teaching a blind child. Anxiety or worry that you might do the wrong thing. Doubt, feeling that you're just not able, because you are not trained to do this. I felt these same emotions when I learned I would have a blind student in my class the following year.

In order to start to get answers to my questions, I turned to the teacher and classroom assistant in the blind student's present class. Their first piece of advice was to start stashing away papers, papers that I anticipate I would want transcribed into braille. So I made two piles, one to send off to the transcriber and one for me to keep, so I could keep track of what was sent out. Whatever I thought I'd need, I collected week by week and put them into a folder. They were returned to me that way by the transcribers. My organization helped their organization. And being organized relieved me— now I could teach everyone who would be in my class.

Next, I read. I read as much as I could. I found terms like contractions, well, we have contractions in English, what's the difference? Second grade level braille, well second grade, she's coming to third grade, you mean there's only second grade braille? No, no, no, that's just the term. So those are the kind of things I was able to ask about and find out about.

Finally, I felt I needed to go into the second grade classroom and observe. I was a little nervous. How did the teacher and the class relate? How does the teacher relate to an assistant at the same time as she's teaching? How do the other children relate to the blind student? How does he relate to the other children? How does he relate to the teacher and the assistant? As I watched, many of my anxious questions began to melt away.

I wondered how I would communicate very visual things. I started thinking that one of the aims we have as teachers is to get our children to communicate orally, to discuss, to get everyone communicating better. The teacher isn't the only one teaching in the classroom. The children would learn to express themselves more clearly, to tell, to explain what it is they see. What a gift for them! And they'd be doing it not just because J. needs to see but because they need to see, too.

As I went further into this whole process, I thought the best way to understand was to get to know the child I was going to teach. I had never worked with a blind child; I had never really known a blind person, so there had to be a lot of things that I needed to know.

So I went to J.'s house during the summer and I met Mom and I met J.'s sister, and I got a chance to observe the fine adjustments that were made. I got to play with J. outside—he taught me bocce. I got to play with his sister, too, who also plays with J. Gee, never thought about that. Got to eat lunch with J. Went out for pizza with the kids. Didn't really know what I was doing, but I was willing to try. Well, it didn't take much trying because I realized J. knew what he was doing. I started to feel a whole lot better because I found one of those secrets I was trying to uncover. It was that J. was more like me and you than not like me and you.

Then the philosophy unveiled itself. I've got to get him to be what he wants to be. I've got to bring out the best in him. He had the feelings, the drive, the moods, the wants, the needs, the expectations, all the many emotions that we all have. And I realized I was dealing with a child and not a disability. That was the stepping stone, that was the key that gave me the impetus to go for it. I was going to expect of him what I expected of every single child in my classroom. It was not that he was so different and there were things he couldn't do. It was "I've got to teach him. I've got to teach him what I'm teaching everyone else." Maybe I've got to make adjustments but he needs to know everything everyone else needs to know. I wouldn't be driven by the thought that he can't do certain things. Then I suddenly realized that had always been my philosophy. I have it hanging on my wall every year—a poster that says, "Say, yes, I can do it!" There it was in the biggest letters staring at me year after year after year—yes, I can do it. This is my own philosophy but I had forgotten that. J. made me realize it again.

—Bebe Facciani
Third Grade Teacher

NEVER GIVE UP ON A CHILD

My student presents an interesting challenge. She is blind and she is also autistic. When I started looking for information on this, I discovered that the way children who are blind learn is very different from the way that children on the autism spectrum learn. Typically children who are blind/visually impaired learn from the part to the whole. For example, they learn that a dot is a symbol for a letter, then what that letter means, and then to put one letter together with another letter, and then eventually that this word means "cat." Children with autism don't typically learn that way. They will see the whole word and every time they see that, they will say that's cat. They are wholistic learners and they tend to be visual which brings us to a problem if you're working with a kid who is also visually impaired or blind. And by visual I mean that most of the things that are presented to these kids are done in picture form.

So where do we go with teaching? We have a child with a disability that encompasses social, behavioral, and processing difficulties, who doesn't fit into the highly visual autism learning style, and therefore the teaching approaches don't work. We wanted to use the Applied Behavioral Analysis technique and discrete trial format which are very systematic and consistent and work well with children on the autism spectrum, but there was very little out there for us to draw on in terms of using this method with a blind student.

Through trial and error and a team effort—teacher, Child Study Team, aide, parents, therapists, braille teacher, O&M Instructor—we synthesized a teaching approach.

The student had a difficult time in terms of time and space—what's happening, where am I going, what's coming up next. So one of the things we did was to structure the classroom very specifically so that activities happened in a certain area. For example, our student learned that the Circle Time activity happened at the circle table. It was very concrete. When it was group time, we went to the group table. Group only happened at one particular table and that was the only activity that happened there. Playtime only happened in the play area. That helped the child in the classroom.

Transitioning is difficult for our student. We wanted to give her a way to know what transition was coming up, when it was coming up, and exactly what the activity was. We made her a very concrete schedule box with real objects attached with Velcro that she could take off and look at in her hands—a little wooden circle table for circle time, a little snack bag for snack time, push pins for her braille readiness program, blocks for indoor recess. As the student progressed, we changed the objects. When it was time for the activity, the object went onto the schedule box and when it was done it went into the all done box.

Then we progressed to a strip of Velcro at the edge of the student's desk. We would put the objects on the Velcro; we didn't have to use the boxes anymore. Once the braille kicked in, we started fading out the little objects and went to a braille schedule and now, I'm happy to say, the student comes in and is able to go through the schedule orally with the rest of the class.

Mobility was another challenge—how to get from point A to point B independently. That was a big goal for us. A lot of times the typical strategies didn't work. We couldn't say, "Don't forget, the water fountain is at the end of the hall." Well, we could, but no matter how many times we said it, the student would still walk into the water fountain. It wasn't meaningful, didn't stay in there, wouldn't process, whatever it was, it wasn't going in. So we needed to do a little extra.

We did things like, for every three steps of independent walking, the student would get a primary reinforcement. At that time the primary reinforcement was—Cocoa Puffs! And then we increased it to five steps, then ten steps, then down to the water fountain, then to the office. We worked toward fading the Cocoa Puffs and giving praise instead. We got to the point where the walking, the mobility part, was really good, but the orientation was not always there. So the O&M Instructor came in again and the whole team sat down to develop a program. We gave her specific areas to go to by herself. The goal was for her to learn to use the environment and natural cues and learn when it was time to ask for directions.

We also used rhythm and songs to work on independent mobility. We made up little rhymes with directions for various places. For example, for walking back from the library, we said: Out the library door we go, across to the wall, make a left, go down the hall, nice and straight and tall. We had one for going to and one for getting back from each place. Before we knew it, she learned all about the hallways saying these little rhymes and could get there by herself.

We found we had to train others in the building. People see a cute little kid with a white cane walking down the hallway and everyone runs to help. Doors magically open. People escort her, carry her books. That's how it is out there. So one of the things I asked right at the beginning was, please do not stop and socialize. When you see another student, do you stop the whole class and say, "Oh, hi, Johnny, how are you?" No, you're only doing it with the blind student. It's very nice, thank you, but don't do it! Know what is appropriate. Ask yourself, do other teachers do this with all other students, or are they only doing it with my blind student?

When we got started with academics, it was functional. What did this student need for her immediate environment and what would she need for her next environment. When we started, we were looking at things like, the child needs to sit in a chair for three seconds. That's where we started, sitting in a chair for three seconds. Then we extended it to five seconds and then we extended it some more.

Eventually, attending behaviors were established—sitting in the chair, quiet head, hands quiet, ready to work. We began to work on prebraille and braille, again using discrete trials. We rewrote the Patterns program and put the Mangold into trials format. The itinerant teacher used the same materials and kept data. Then we sent those things home for homework and the parents worked on it at home. We're at the point now where our student can do on command reading of sentences, sight words, and word families.

If we got stuck, we'd meet with the team again, look at the situation again, and try something else. We decided to rewrite the reading program, because it wouldn't work for this student. We ended up over the course of seven years, rewriting the reading program four times. We tried different presentations, different ways of doing things. When something stopped working, we'd look at it again and try something else.

You may have a challenging student, too. Getting that student ready to learn does not take a couple of weeks. It doesn't even take a couple of months. It takes a couple of years. But never give up on the child. Hang in there, be consistent, and it will come.

—Irene Cook
Special Education Teacher

EVERYTHING IS GEARED TOWARD INDEPENDENCE

I am a classroom aide for a child who is now in second grade. When I first began working with P., in preschool, I had no idea what I was doing. It was also the teacher's first year with a blind or visually impaired student. I was told not to worry and that I would be amazed at what he was capable of and daily, he amazes me.

In the beginning, P. did not have a cane, a CCTV, or braille. The first adapted items we had for him were a slant board and a high-intensity light. During that first year the TVI brought in a CCTV. That was a learning experience. It was pretty difficult to learn how to move the tray and to read at the same time. We started out with the print alphabet. Then we drew circles using the CCTV. Learning how to manipulate the tray was very difficult for P. He also has ADD which interferes with his keeping on track. He'd play with the knobs on the CCTV and move the tray all over the place. He did manage to master it. He's very good at it now.

After the first year of preschool, P. started to learn braille. He was using the CCTV for reading and he was also learning to read braille. All of these skills were difficult for him because of his ADD, his fine motor problems, and his visual impairment.

I went along on lessons with the mobility instructor and the PE specialist who both gave us lots of ideas. I would also go with P. to occupational therapy so I could learn the techniques. PT, gym class, I went to them all. In the classroom, I work with the other children, too, but in the specials, I worked with P. At lunchtime, I taught him how to open his lunchbox, open the milk carton, all the skills he needed to function in the cafeteria. I helped him interact and learn how to play with the other children.

Now P. is in a regular second grade. I do not stay with him at lunch any more. He manages fine by himself. This year he takes medication and needs to look at his watch. At 12:30 I go out and make sure he remembered. He's now responsible for looking at his watch and at 12:30, finding an aide on the playground, telling her he's now going in to the nurse to take his medication, going in and taking the medication, then going back outside and telling the aide he's back.

Everything we do is geared toward independence—getting the child to be efficient and independent. It doesn't happen overnight. It takes a lot of hard work, persistence, and imagination, and a lot of people working together sharing their ideas. If something doesn't work one way, maybe someone else has a better idea. We have to keep our minds open and try new approaches so that the student keeps making progress.

—Winnie Elberson
Classroom Aide

BLINDNESS WAS JUST ANOTHER CHARACTERISTIC

There were a number of things that made our year in science class successful, but very few of them were anything special that I did because of my student's blindness. Someone once advised me to treat this student "just like everyone else." But there is no such thing as "everyone else." Every student presents a unique set of circumstances and teachers must respond to each student as an individual.

When I organize lab groups, for example, I take many things into account—personality, behavior, reactions, abilities, gender—for all my students. Blindness was just another characteristic I took into consideration. I would put my blind student into a group with "givers," patient students who enjoyed being helpful. I also made sure each student had a job to do in the group. If a group didn't work out, I switched kids, but I keep an eye on that for all my students. I did seat the student near my desk so that when I demonstrated equipment, I could casually put it down on his desk for him to examine. It also helped that both he and I were organized.

The onus is on the teacher to respond in an appropriate way to every child's situation. The onus is on the child to be an independent learner, to pay attention and do the work and come to me if he or she needs help. This is the case for a blind student and for any student.

—Madeline Sinoway
Eighth Grade Science Teacher

MAKE IT SUCCESSFUL FOR EVERY CHILD

My basic philosophy in teaching students whether sighted or non, is that every one of us has a handicap of some sort. Therefore we have to adapt our curriculum in some manner on a day-to-day basis, on a month-to-month basis, in whatever particular sport or activity we're involved in, to make it successful for every child.

The first thing I did when I learned I would have a totally blind student in my class was visit her at her elementary school. I observed how her PE teacher there was integrating her into every activity. I also attended any workshops available on inclusion techniques.

With each of our sports and activities at the junior high school, my first question to my student was, had she ever felt anything, any diagrams in braille or raised lines for any of the sports—the outline of a soccer field, the outline of a football field. We now have a whole booklet in braille and raised lines with information for each sport and activity we have been involved in. That booklet will go on with her to the high school.

Next is equipment and adaptation. We use balls and beepers that are available for the blind; some equipment I adapted myself. We've found out that the bell ball works very well for soccer. For practicing individual skills for basketball the bell ball works well, although it's a little bit heavy and awkward, so we ended up using the regular ball for that. We've used the Zoomball. The kids love it. We time each other and see how quickly they can pull it back and forth. They have a lot of fun with that. We've used jumpropes, regular and the one that has beads on it so you can hear the sound. Sometimes we leave it right on the floor and just have the students jump over it. We work with partners. We've used tape lines on the floor, a beeper, we've clapped back and forth.

My blind student is a part of every one of our sports. Either independently, with a partner, or with myself, she is actively participating. She'll do the soccer throw in. In basketball, she'll run up and down the court with a partner and inbound for both teams. She inbounds the ball with a chest pass. As we're running down the court, I'm constantly giving verbal cues. So-and-so has the ball, they just made the shot, rebounded, we've got to make a U-turn, ball's off to your right, ball's straight ahead, ball's coming to your left. The verbal gives the visual.

We go over body mechanics on how to release the ball, body mechanics on soccer, how to kick it inside, outside, same thing that is required by students who are sighted. I buddy her up with someone to catch a pass. The cue is "incoming." She catches it and had learned not to catch it on the chest.

Centering in football, she did that. She's done the handoff. For volleyball, we've used a beachball, a lighter weight ball. She can get it over the net. So she's been included and has taken part in every one of the classes. She does the exercises with all the rest of the students. Some of the kids in all my classes do more or less and that is no problem to me or to any of the students, whatsoever

We just started kickball using the beeper. Another student sets the beeper up on the base and my blind student uses it as a guide and goes around the bases without a partner. The ball is rolled to her or we set it up for her. She gives it a good kick. We made the rule that the ball has to be passed to three people first before they try to get her out. Meanwhile she's running toward the beeper at first base. When we stop the beeper, she knows she's on the base. The other student moves on to the next base with the beeper. After the next person up kicks, she runs towards the beeper again.

I tried using the beeper on the backstop also. It does work. You just have to lower the backstop so the beeper can be heard. In a class of fifty some odd students in an older small gymnasium with lots of balls moving around, it's noisy. When we work on individual skills, we take a barrel, go to one section of the gym, and have a student there or myself. We use a hand or a plastic board as a backboard. She chest passes into the barrel. She hears if it hits the rim and bounces out. She knows, oops, didn't make my two points that time. She has to count and have the same number of tries as the sighted students for taking a lay-up shot. She counts them up, gives me the score, just like everybody else.

For soccer we used a partner or myself. The ball comes to us, we pass it to somebody else, or we're on the sideline and my student inbounds. The others clap to let her know where they are, same thing as basketball, and she passes the ball to them. She knows where the goal is. She's played defense, she's played offense. She knows the skills—passing, trapping, inbounding. She knows the rules, has the full diagram of the field.

One of my special goals for this student this year was to improve upon physical fitness. This is part of our curriculum. This year we accomplished two things in this area. The first was for her to do the 50-yard dash by herself using a guide wire. A person stood at each end clapping, then she just used the baton right down the middle and ran toward the noise. She did exceptionally well. I think she really enjoyed the independence in that activity and that is part of it. The other thing was doing the mile. She has just completed the mile and did exceptionally well.

She uses her cane well. She has the full pattern for getting around the locker room. Next year she'll have to learn the high school, but hopefully, she'll gain the same confidence with that. It will be a new experience, as it was when she came here from a small elementary school. We have two levels in the building. We do have an elevator, but she uses the stairs all the time. She'll have several levels of stairs to do next year at the high school, so she'll get extra physical fitness that way, too. I have confidence that she'll do just fine.

—Linda Kent
Junior High School Physical Education Teacher

I HAVE ONLY ONE REGRET

First of all, I am not an expert on the blind. I'm really a student learning like everybody else is. When I first heard that I was going to be teaching a blind student I was very concerned. I had no experience in dealing with a blind individual—ever—much less a student that I was going to be teaching. I explained my concerns to my department head. He said, "Don't worry. It's going to work out well." I wasn't so sure.

My second concern was the physical logistics of the room. How would I deal with this? Where would I seat C.? If C. had to leave the room, how would I deal with that and also teach my other students at the same time? This was her first year in the high school. I was concerned about her knowing the layout of the building. How would I manage that situation? Also, I had my students working in cooperative learning teams. There would be a lot of moving around the room. C. would have to get up and move in all directions. The physical was a big concern to me.

Another concern was relationships with other students in the class. Would they work together well? I had no experience with a blind student before and I didn't know what to expect in this area. I didn't know if the other students would receive her well, if she'd receive them well, or what the situation would be.

Learning materials—where would the learning materials come from for a blind student. I didn't have any. I knew the Social Studies department didn't have any. I wasn't aware that the school system had any at all, so that was another concern.

A further concern was the fact that we had a brand new curriculum. This was an enriched level World History, a brand new course. We had worked for about five years redesigning the entire course. It would no longer be a traditional course taught in chronological order from the Stone Age to whenever it ended. It was going to be completely restructured. Everything was going to be new. We had written up unit plans the previous year but we had no specific lesson plans yet. So, my concern was how would I be able to produce lesson plans for a new course for a new class and also at the same time, perhaps several lesson plans for a student who is blind.

My last major concern regarded graphic materials—maps, graphs, charts, etc. How would I be able to use those in the class? How would I be able to use visuals in the class, if I had a student who wasn't going to be able to see them?

How did it all turn out? I ended up using just plain common sense and flexibility. That seemed to work pretty much where my lack of experience was a problem. As far as actually dealing with a blind person, I just decided it would be a learning experience. I knew that I would probably do well in some areas and I would probably make some mistakes in others and that I would be learning at the same time. I just accepted that fact.

Regarding the logistics of the room, I tried to apply common sense. I seated C. in the first seat in the first row. She could easily find the seat when she came in and it was a clear path to the door when she needed to leave the room. Regarding the layout of the building, I subsequently found out that C. had been in the building the previous summer, mapping out the layout of the corridors. Our building is a big maze and she had been walking around, so she already had the layout of the building to some degree.

C. was in her art class just before she had history, and the art classroom is all the way up at the other end of the building. I thought I would have to make arrangements to give her a little extra time to get to my class. Quite frankly, C. got to the class before most of my other students.

As far as moving students into cooperative learning teams, at first I made a mistake. I asked the other students to come and sit where C. was sitting. Then very politely, C. said, please don't do that. I can go to wherever my group is. So what we did after that was have her move around the room to whatever team she was going to be a member of on that particular day and the students just automatically helped her get there.

Relations with other students—how did they get along? They did. Most students knew C. They'd been in school with her for years. They worked well with her. The fear was really mine. The students knew how to deal with the situation. Another thing I have to say is that C. really knew how to take care of herself. She's very assertive and you don't mess with C. If you do, she's going to let you know about it!

We did have one situation when a student made an unkind remark. I feel that that's the same as making a racial or an ethnic remark or a religious remark and I promptly sent the student to the office. The vice principal dealt with the situation. The student had to write an essay and we had a long talk with him. I subsequently had a problem with that same student making a remark about someone else, so we really had to stay on top of that and let the student know that that was not proper behavior.

Regarding the learning materials, we had a problem right from the word go because our textbook was not in braille and we couldn't get it in braille. We did have the audiotape, but it didn't work well with the way we used the book in groups. So in class we had students read to C., which worked well in our cooperative learning teams. The dynamics of the groups were good.

Regarding the new curriculum—that put the pressure on. Making new materials for a new course and a new class and making new worksheets that would also work with a blind person tested my abilities. Our school hired someone to produce braille and adapt materials for C., so the plan was for me to get the worksheets to our transcriber daily. I was creating them as we went along and usually I was working through lunch to get them done so that they could be transcribed into braille by period 8, when C. had her class. We were able to get most of them into braille and into the classroom on time. On a couple of occasions I was late and what we did was dictate the set of questions or whatever it was to C. and she would type the answers on her little computer and that took care of that situation very well.

Graphic materials—this was the area of most difficulty. Our transcriber was able to produce maps with raised lines so that you could feel the borders of a country, for example, but I found that for this history course where a lot of the historical locations had different names, that didn't work very well. On the positive side, though, most of our map assignments had to do with analysis—not just where Rome is located or where Carthage is located, but what groups of people were located in a certain area, what natural resources were available, and so on. The assignments involved a lot of analysis in the cooperative learning teams, so I found that I didn't worry too much if C. didn't know geographically exactly where a city was located. But if she could understand the dynamics of the natural resources, how the characteristics of the land affected the history, how the people had been fighting over land—if she understood what the problems were, I felt that that was more important than knowing exactly where a particular city was located.

This was a real learning experience for me. I never thought in my thirty-two years of teaching that I'd ever be teaching a blind student. I got a lot out of it. Things worked out quite well. Many factors had to do with why it worked out well. One is that C. is extremely independent. She worked very hard. She asked for help when she needed it, but she is actually much more self-reliant than most of my other students. Another factor is that C. is a very acute listener. She hears and she digests information better than many students. Maybe they are distracted, looking around the room. I remember one day there was a power failure at the high school. All the students were saying, "The lights are out, the lights are out." C.'s remark was, "What's the big deal!" Because C. listened better than my other students, she was able to discuss better than other students. I did choose my words carefully, to make sure I was using precise language.

Another help in class was the fact that C. used that little computer and was able to take all the information and notes down and then print out whatever was necessary on a printer. Another help was my students. I guess by this time, they've learned how to get along with others. I found that most of my students were helpful and cooperative. One in particular worked with her a lot, read to her a lot. He was more than a help—he really cared.

Another factor that helped was that we were working in cooperative learning teams which required a lot of thinking, analyzing, discussing, synthesizing. The visual factor was not paramount.

I thoroughly enjoyed working with C. She worked harder than most of my students. She always took part in discussions and we always enjoyed hearing her viewpoints. She has a lot of opinions about things. She always maintained a sense of humor in class, which everybody enjoyed. This was one of my most enjoyable teaching experiences. I have only one regret—that I won't have C. in class next year.

—Michael Gialanella
High School History Teacher

AN INDEPENDENT FULL PARTICIPANT

One day the Director of Special Services in our school district called me and said that a parent wanted to enroll an age-appropriate child in one of our Kindergartens. A bit perplexed, I said, "What's the problem?" The Director responded by informing me that the child was blind. I asked if he meant legally blind—having some vision. "No," he said, "this child has absolutely no sight." Before hanging up the phone, we discussed the many roadblocks that we would face in trying to educate such a child. After all, how could we ever meet the needs of a blind child within a regular elementary school setting? No one on staff had any training or experience with such a child. Indeed, it sounded as if it would be an impossible fit. Wouldn't she be better off in a setting more suitable to her unique needs?

Soon after this, the child's mother called and made an appointment to see me. I sat with this parent for nearly two hours, talking with her, but mostly listening to her thoughts on how a blind child could find success in public school. At the end of our meeting, I easily concluded that this was the most impassioned mom that I had ever met. Her persuasive arguments were centered on the premise that a blind child is not helpless and with simple accommodations, can achieve almost anything that a sighted child can achieve. The mom's sense of confidence coupled with an impressive knowledge of "blindness" had a dramatic impact upon me. I seemed to feel, if not catch, her passion.

The night after the conference I tossed and turned, knowing that this parent had really affected me. Although I still wasn't sure if the placement was doable, I knew we had to try. At the office the next morning, I called the Director of Special Services and suggested a call to the agency that would send the Teacher of the Visually Impaired for starters. Then we set up a meeting with the parents. I stressed the need to "allow" this mom to help and guide us.

My next step was to convince the principal. After all, the principal is the instructional leader of the school. If the principal is aboard, it will work; if the principal doesn't buy in, failure is just about inevitable. The principal was very willing to try. Meetings with the teacher, principal, Director, IEP Team, and parents ensued. I functioned behind the scenes as a cheerleader and facilitator. The student had a successful year in kindergarten. Her teacher was willing to learn, listen and work.

The Teacher of the Visually Impaired was an important part of our team approach. Our teachers were great. I recall how the physical education instructor had the student shooting baskets, using a can with a sound beeper to give her an auditory sense of where to aim. She played regular baseball, too, partnering in the field with sighted kids. Indeed, she attended all regular classes with the assistance of a full-time aide, who was no longer in the room by third grade. By that time the aide worked primarily on converting the academic work into braille.

The student is now in high school. She takes advanced levels of English and History, along with regular Algebra, Earth Science, and Spanish. She even participates in all science labs with accommodations, when necessary. There is no aide. I might add that she plays a mean bongo drum as a member of the high school jazz band.

As an educational leader, I initially suffered from "sighted bias." I automatically thought that blind people needed an inordinate amount of help and could never lead a normal school existence. Boy, was I wrong. The student's mom taught me a lot, most significantly that blind people can accomplish just about anything a sighted person can do. I also learned that teachers and administrators willing to be creative and sensitive can help blind children accomplish and meet all their goals and aspirations. Last but not least, our student taught us that a blind child can become an independent, full participant in any classroom.

—Dr. Lawrence Feinsod
Superintendent of Schools

I'VE NEVER SEEN A CHILD WHO DOESN'T HAVE A GIFT

The administrator needs to match the personality of the student with the personality of the teacher. Will they understand each other? Do they share values? Capitalize on staff who are willing to try something new, willing to take a risk, willing to go the extra mile. Pick a teacher who understands that learning can be measured in many ways, not just with traditional paper and pencil.

Everybody learns differently. We need to assess students in ways that make it possible for them to show us what they have learned. I see it as the responsibility of the teacher to assess the student appropriately and the responsibility of the administrator to counsel teachers so that they are comfortable doing this. Administrators also need to work with the writers of the IEP to make sure it is specific regarding assessment and then to make sure the IEP is realized.

The school has to provide the student with an education the child can use in the future, a practical education that is suited to the child's interests and abilities. You've got to partner with the parents about the direction the child wants to go in and then choose courses that will help the student go in that direction. Look at the curriculum. Look at the courses. Match the student with teachers who will help the student achieve his goals. Then move classes around, change the master schedule if necessary, so that you can put the student with the right teachers.

It's the job of the teacher to capitalize on the positive traits and strengths of the student—every student. It's the job of the administrator to provide an atmosphere in which this will happen. I haven't met one kid in thirty years who wasn't a genius at something and who didn't have a disability at something—and that goes right up to the valedictorians. We have to address students as individuals and bring each one to his fullest potential.

We can't treat everyone exactly alike, according to some rigid standard. For the child with special needs, we have to make legitimate accommodations so that he can reach his fullest potential. We also have to insist that the student with special needs gets every opportunity that every other student gets. If that means making some changes, then we should make them and not make a big deal of it.

A principal has to provide an atmosphere in which teachers can teach and students can learn. I treat my faculty the way I want them to treat the students—with kindness, with respect. I try to treat each one as an individual, according to what his or her needs are. And that's how they should treat the kids. There's something in every kid that you can like—there's something in every person that you can like. If we appreciate the people who come into our lives and learn from them, life can be a lot more interesting and fun.

The goals for the student have to be appropriate. We want the kids to find success. Yet the students shouldn't feel so comfortable that they never have to work at overcoming an obstacle. We want to smooth the path for them so that they have a chance, but not smooth it so much that they won't be prepared for real life. If they meet success ninety percent of the time and difficulty ten percent of the time, then they have the opportunity to learn to overcome obstacles or failure. If we shelter a child from every possible thing that could go wrong, we are doing the child a disservice because he won't learn how to cope.

We cannot pretend to know what experiences parents have had with their children. They know their kids, they've been through what doesn't work, they know what works. We should listen to them! I think administrators should invite parents in before school even starts for an introductory meeting. Then say to them, you've lived with this kid for X years, tell us what works. So we can start there and not have to lose a year experimenting. The parent can hand you a blueprint of how the child learns, good tips, good insights on what works. And to parents, if the administration does not invite you in, make the suggestion.

Don't be afraid of the student with special needs. Don't worry that you'll offend if you say the wrong thing or embarrass the child if you call on him and he gives the wrong answer. It's okay for the student to be wrong and it's okay to ask questions. Just ask without malice.

I've never seen a child who doesn't have a disability and I've never seen a child who doesn't have a gift. It's up to the team to get the best out of the child by teaching the child to compensate for the disability and to work with the gift.

—R. Bruce Padian
High School Principal

RESOURCES

Products with the color, contrast, tactile, and auditory characteristics that will work well with blind/visually impaired children can be found in regular stores and catalogues. In addition, many companies sell products made specifically for blind/VI people. This section will help you find them.

Following is a list of items useful for the classroom and school, some that you can find in regular stores and catalogs and some that are specialty products. Sources appear after the list.

Adapting Materials
- Wikki Stix
- Hi-Mark
- T-shirt markers
- Colored glue
- Tracing wheel
- Coloring screen—see page 155
- Sewell Kit
- Swail Dot Inverter
- Self-stick textures
- Velcro
- Wooden craft pieces
- Drafting tape

Making It Work: Educating the Blind/VI Student in the Regular School, 187–213
Copyright © 2005 by Information Age Publishing

- Cardboard
- String
- Double-sided tape
- Braille labeler
- Labeling tape
- Laminating sheets

General Classroom Use

- Feelable/scented stickers
- Magnets and magnet board
- Push pins and corkboard
- Raised-line coloring books
- Non-roll crayons
- Scented clay
- Braille/large print watch
- Talking watch/clock
- Tactile/large print timer

Reading/Writing

- Braillewriter
- Braillewriter pad
- Braille paper
- Shelf for over braillewriter
- Holding tray
- Dycem
- Oversize folders
- Braille cheat sheet
- Franklin Language Master Special Edition
- Markers
- Heavy line paper
- Book stand
- Acetate sheets
- Magnifiers
- Braille/large print Dolch cards
- Braille phonics practice sheets

Math

- Braille/large print flashcards
- Tactily-marked Unifix cubes (create using self-stick textures)

- Tactile practice clock
- Fraction kits
- Raised-line/heavy-line graph paper
- Talking/large print scientific calculator
- Solid geometric forms
- Tactile/large print measuring equipment
- Tactile/large print geometry materials
- Nemeth Code cheat sheet
- Tactile dice

Social Studies
- Relief map
- Tactile globe
- Braille maps
- Braille atlas

Science
- Chemistry/biology/anatomy models
- Land forms
- Tactile science diagrams
- Tactile astronomy diagrams and books

Art
- Sight, sound, touch art books
- Tactile art project books

P.E./Recess
- Bell balls
- Beeper balls
- Beepers
- Sound source
- Zoom ball
- Jumpropes
- Hippity Hop ball

Games
- Braille/large print playing cards
- Braille/large print Uno

- Braille/large print Bingo
- Braille/large print Monopoly
- Braille/print Scrabble
- Tactile Connect 4
- Tactile Checkers
- Chess
- Talking Battleship
- Bop-It
- Simon

EDUCATION MATERIALS

American Printing House for the Blind (APH)
1839 Frankfort Ave.
PO Box 6085
Louisville, KY 40206-0085
1-800-223-1839
www.aph.org

> The major producer of instructional and educational materials for blind/VI children from infancy through prevocational; includes items for literacy, math, science, geography, etc., adapted testing materials, books, games.

Creative Adaptations for Learning (CAL)
38 Beverly Rd.
Great Neck, NY 11021-1330
516-466-9143
www.cal-s.org

> Raised-line drawings and learning materials.

Exceptional Teaching Aids
20102 Woodbine Ave.
Castro Valley, CA 94546
1-800-549-6999
www.exceptionalteaching.com

> Materials for education, recreation, and independent living.

Franklin Electronic Publishers
One Franklin Plaza
Burlington, NJ 08016-4907
1-800-266-5626
www.franklin.com

Speaking Language Master dictionary.

Howe Press
Perkins School for the Blind
175 No. Beacon St.
Watertown, MA 02472
617-924-3434
www.perkins.org

Perkins braillewriter, slates and styluses, math aids.

IntelliTools
1720 Corporate Circle
Petaluma, CA 94954
1-800-899-6687
www.intellitools.com

Products can be adapted for use with blind/VI students.

Lilli Nielsen Materials
Books and materials created by Lilli Nielsen, internationally known
teacher of blind children, especially children with significant delays or
additional disabilities; feature active learning approach to stimulate
development in all areas. Available from:

LilliWorks	**Vision Associates**
1815 Encinal Ave.	2109 US Hwy 90 West Ste. 170 #312
Almeda, CA 94501	Lake City, FL 32055
510-814-9111	407-352-1200
www.lilliworks.com	www.visionkits.com

NFB-NEWSLINE
National Center for the Blind
1800 Johnson St.
Baltimore, MD 21230
410-659-9314
www.nfb.org/newsline1.htm

Free daily access to a variety of newspapers and magazines over the telephone; ready at 6 a.m.; call National Center to register and receive ID number and security code.

Nienhuis Montessori USA
140 E. Dana St.
Mountain View, CA 94041-1576
1-800-942-8697
www.nienhuis-usa.com

Educational and independent living materials.

North Coast Medical
18305 Sutter Blvd.
Morgan Hill, CA 95037-2845
1-800-821-9319
www.ncmedical.com

Dycem–nonslip material (place on work area so that pages or other items won't slip).

Jackson Education Service District
Attn: Oregon Project
101 No. Grape St.
Medford, OR 97501
1-800-636-7450
www.jacksonesd.k12.or.us/sectionindex.asp?sectionid=132

Publishes the *Oregon Project*, a skills inventory with teaching activities for blind/VI children birth to six.

National Resource Center for Blind Musicians
Music and Arts Center for Humanity
510 Barnum Ave. 3rd fl.
Bridgeport, CT 06601
203-366-3300
www.blindmusicstudent.org

Information on sources of braille music, technology, how to include blind students in music; training for teachers and students.

Princeton Braillists
76 Leabrook La.
Princeton, NJ 08540
609-924-5207
215-357-7715

Raised-line maps and drawings excellent for school use.

Washington State School for the Blind
2214 E. 13 St.
Vancouver, WA 98661-4120
360-696-6321
www.wssb.org

Accessible software downloads for use with IntelliTools.

SCIENCE

Carolina Biological Supply Co.
2700 York Rd.
Burlington, NC 27215-3398
1-800-334-5551
www.carolina.com

Hands-on models for biology, chemistry, etc.

Childbirth Graphics
PO Box 21207
Waco, TX 76702-1207
1-800-299-3366
www.childbirthgraphics.com

Hands-on internal organs; childbirth and general health catalogs.

Jernigan Institute Science Academy
National Federation of the Blind
1800 Johnson St.
Baltimore, MD 21230
410-659-9314
www.nfb.org/nfbrti/science_academy.htm

Summer science experiences for blind/VI students.

National Braille Press
88 St. Stephen St.
Boston, MA 02115-4302
1-800-548-7323
www.nbp.org

Publishes *Touch the Stars I and II*.

National Acadamies Press
500 Fifth St. NW
Lockbox 285
Washington, DC 20055
1-888-624-8373
www.nap.edu/catalog/10307.html

> Publishes *Touch the Universe.*

Future Reflections
www.nfb.org

> Volume 23, Number 1, Spring/Summer 2004 issue contains many resources
> in tactile form for the study of astronomy.

TAEVIS Online
Purdue University, Office of the Dean of Students
302 Wood St.
West Lafayette IN 47907-2108
765-496-2856
www.taevisonline.purdue.edu

> An electronic library of thousands of tactile science diagrams to purchase.
> Made to work with tactile image makers (see Tactile Graphics, below).

ART

Art Education for the Blind
160 Mercer St.
NY, NY 10012
212-334-3700
www.artseducation.info

> Publishes *Art Beyond Sight* and *Art History through Touch and Sound;* provides
> hands-on and audio museum programs.

TACTILE GRAPHICS

Several machines can be used to create tactile graphics. Use caution, however, that the final product is legible to the fingers! The following two
companies make machines that use heat and special paper to create
raised-line drawings from print originals.

Pulse Data Humanware
175 Mason Circle
Concord, CA 94520
1-800-722-3393
www.humanware.com

Manufactures Pictures in a Flash (PIAF).

Repro-Tronics
75 Carver Ave.
Westwood, NJ 07675
800-948-8453
www.repro-tronics.com

Manufactures the Tactile Image Enhancer (TIE).

ViewPlus Technologies
1853 SW Airport Ave.
Corvallis, OR 97333
1-866-836-2184
www.viewplustech.com

Produces the high-end Powered by Tiger line of braille embossers which can create tactile images from pictures, clip art, drawings, Internet graphics, etc.

Future Reflections
www.nfb.org

Volume 22, Number 3, Fall 2003 issue contains resources for tactile materials.

BOOKS IN BRAILLE, RECORDED, AND ELECTRONIC FORM

American Printing House for the Blind (APH)
1839 Frankfort Ave.
PO Box 6085
Louisville, KY 40206-0085
1-800-223-1839
www.aph.org

Textbooks and some fiction in braille, large print, tape, and downloadable formats. Also braille readiness and early literacy books. Newsweek and Reader's Digest in braille, tape, and disk. Louis Accessible Materials database lists books in all alternative formats (see Searchable Databases, below).

Bookshare.org
www.bookshare.org

Electronic books for downloading from the Internet; small membership fee, but can search database free of charge (see Searchable Databases, below).

Braille Circulating Library
2700 Stuart Ave.
Richmond, VA 23220-3305
804-359-3743
www.careministries.org/bcl.html

Christian books (some fiction) in braille, large print, and tape.

Braille Institute
741 No. Vermont Ave.
Los Angeles, CA 90029
1-800-BRAILLE (1-800-272-4553)
www.brailleinstitute.org

Expectations and *Brailleways* annual anthologies of children's literature; Braille Special Collection catalog offering four free books three times per year.

Braille International
3290 SE Slater St.
Stuart, FL 34997
772-286-8366
www.brailleintl.org

William A. Thomas Braille Bookstore; braille leisure books through the mail; braille jewelry.

Braille Resource and Literacy Center
(BRL Center)
1094 So 350 West
Orem, UT 84058
801-224-3334
www.brlcenter.org

Beginning reader books in Grade 1 (uncontracted) braille with print; children's books in Grade 2 braille with print.

Braille Superstore
1-800-987-DOTS (1-800-987-1231)
www.braillebookstore.com

Braille books for children and adults; games, toys.

Catholic Guild for the Blind
180 No. Michigan Ave., Suite 1700
Chicago, IL 60601
312-236-8569
www.guildfortheblind.org

Tactile-picture coloring books; book on making pictures using braille dots; some fiction books.

Christian Record Services
4444 So. 52 St.
PO Box 6097
Lincoln, NB 68506-0097
402-488-0981
www.christianrecord.org

General and religious books, magazines.

Kenneth Jernigan Library for Blind Children
American Action Fund for Blind Children and Adults (AAF)
1800 Johnson St.
Baltimore, MD 21230
410-659-9314, X 361
www.blindactionfund.org

Lending library of Twin-Vision (print-braille) and braille books; popular series books to keep; Great Documents in braille; braille calendar; newspaper service for deaf-blind people.

Louis Braille Center
320 Dayton St., Suite 125
Edmonds, WA 98020-3590
425-776-4142
www.louisbraillecenter.org

Braille books for purchase; used books free for the asking.

National Braille Press

88 St. Stephen St.
Boston, MA 02115-4302
1-800-548-7323
www.nbp.org

> Braille and print-braille books, calendars, speller, phonics books; Children's Braille Book Club.

National Library Service for the Blind and Physically Handicapped (NLS)

1291 Taylor St., NW
Washington DC 20011
1-800-424-8567
www.loc.gov/nls

> Braille, large-print, and recorded books loaned through state or regional libraries; web-braille service over the Internet; database of books in alterative formats (see Searchable Databases, below); braille music; braille transcriber courses.

Recording for the Blind & Dyslexic (RFB&D)

20 Roszel Rd.
Princeton, NJ 08540
1-800-221-4792
www.rfbd.org

> Textbooks on tape and CD; can search catalog and order online.

Seedlings

PO Box 51924
Livonia, MI 48151-5924
1-800-777-8552
www.seedlings.org

> Braille and print-braille books to purchase for children from preschool through junior high.

Volunteer Braille Service

1710 Douglas Dr.
Golden Valley MN 55422
763-544-2880
www.vbsmn.org

> Very Bumpy Stories, preschool through elementary level books to purchase; library of print-braille books free to individuals all over U.S. and schools/ agencies in MN.

SEARCHABLE DATABASES

Louis Accessible Materials and APH File Repository
www.aph.org/louis.htm

Bookshare.org
www.bookshare.org

National Library Service
http://nlscatalog.loc.gov

> For Web-Braille, contact the state or regional library for the blind to receive a password and login information.

ADAPTIVE AIDS, EQUIPMENT, AND TOYS

Ann Morris Enterprises
PO Box 9022
Hicksville, NY 11802-9022
1-800-537-2118
www.annmorris.com

> Products for the blind/visually impaired.

Independent Living Aids
200 Robbins Lane
PO Box 9022
Jericho, NY 11753
1-800-537-2118
www.independentliving.com

> Products for the blind/visually impaired.

LS & S Group
PO Box 673
Northbrook, IL 60065
1-800-468-4789
www.lssgroup.com

> Products for the blind/visually impaired and hard of hearing.

National Center for the Blind
Aids and Appliances/Materials Center
1800 Johnson St.
Baltimore, MD 21230
410-659-9314
www.nfb.org

   Products for the blind/visually impaired.

New-Vision
919 Walnut St., 1st fl.
Philadelphia, PA 19107
215-629-2990
www.thenewvisionstore.com

   Products for the blind/visually impaired.

Sammons-Preston
270 Remington Blvd. Suite C
Bolingbrook, IL 60440
1-800-323-5547
www.sammonspreston.com

   Rehabilitation supplies.

Science Products
Box 888
Southeastern, PA 19399
1-800-888-7400

   Products for the blind/visually impaired.

Southpaw Enterprises
PO Box 1047
Dayton, OH 45401
1-800-228-1698
www.southpawenterprises.com

   Sensory integration equipment and materials.

Toys for Special Children and **Enabling Devices**
385 Warburton Ave.
Hastings-on-Hudson, NY 10706
1-800-832-8697
www.enablingdevices.com

   Toys and devices for children with physical impairments.

PHYSICAL EDUCATION AND RECREATION

AAHPERD
PO Box 385
Oxon Hill, MD 20750
1-800-321-0789
www.aahperd.org

Books about including students with disabilities in physical education and fitness activities.

Blind Children's Resource Center
www.blindchildren.org

Check the Sports, Games, and Leisure Time section.

Flaghouse
601 Flaghouse Dr.
Hasbrouck Hts., NJ 07604-3116
1-800-793-7900
www.flaghouse.com

Regular and special needs physical education and athletic equipment and rehab supplies.

Sportime
3155 Northwoods Pkwy
Norcross, GA 30071
1-800-283-5700
www.sportime.com

Regular and special needs physical education and athletic equipment.

S & S Worldwide
PO Box 513
Colchester, CT 06415
1-800-243-9232
www.ssww.com

Recreation, athletic, and physical education products.

US Association of Blind Athletes (USABA)
33 No. Institute St.
Colorado Springs, CO 80903
719-630-0422
www.usaba.org

> Competitive and noncompetitive sports opportunities for blind/VI children and adults in alpine and Nordic skiing, goalball, judo, power lifting, swimming, tandem cycling, track and field, and wrestling.

"Physical Education and Recreation for Blind and Visually Impaired Students," by Angelo Montagnino, *Future Reflections*, Winter 2001, Vol. 20 No. 4.

www.nfb.org/

AUDIO DESCRIPTION

Audio description is the verbal describing of plays, movies, television shows, and other events by trained narrators who describe costumes, settings, characters, facial expressions, movements, etc. that would not be visible to a blind or visually impaired viewer. The narration is timed so that it does not interfere with the dialogue, music, or action in the work. The blind/VI patron wears a small earpiece during the performance to hear the description. There is no charge for audio description.

Audio-described *plays* are usually preceded by a Sensory Seminar right before the performance, when blind/VI patrons are able to handle props and costumes and sometimes walk through the stage set. There is no extra charge for the seminar. Check with your local playhouse to see if this service is available.

Descriptive Video Service (DVS) describes many *movies*. Those available on video can be purchased or sometimes borrowed through your state or regional Library for the Blind. DVS also describes some IMAX and first-run films that are playing in theaters. These films can be shown *only in DVS-equipped movie theaters*. When a described movie is playing, no special arrangements have to be made. The blind/VI patron can go to any show on any day and simply ask for a headset at the box office.

Audio-described *television shows* are available for many PBS shows and Turner Classic Movies. To receive the narration, set the television to the SAP (second audio program) feature.

If you assign students to watch a certain show on television, or if you are planning a field trip to a movie or play, check to see if audio description is available.

DVS Home Video
WGBH Educational Foundation
125 Western Ave.
Boston, MA 02134
1-800-333-1203
www.wgbh.org/dvs

> Audio-described movies to purchase; your state or regional Library for the
> Blind may have these available to borrow.

DVS Theatrical
www.mopix.org

> Website lists DVS-equipped large-format and regular movie theaters in vari-
> ous states; also lists described movies that can be seen in theaters.

Hospital Audiences
548 Broadway, 3rd fl.
NY, NY 10012
212-575-7676
www.hospitalaudiences.org

> Information on audio-described Broadway performances.

CHILDREN WITH ADDITIONAL DISABILITIES

Blind Children's Fund
311 W Broadway Suite 1
Mt. Pleasant, MI 48858
989-779-9966
www.blindchildrensfund.org

> Information, resources, and materials to help parents and teachers teach
> and nurture their blind, visually impaired, and multiply disabled children.
> Publishes the *VIP Newsletter.*

Canine Companions for Independence
PO Box 446
Santa Rosa, CA 95402-0446
1-800-572-2275
www.caninecompanions.org

> Dogs trained to assist and enhance the independence of people with physi-
> cal or developmental disabilities.

Inter-American Conductive Education Association (IACEA)
PO Box 3169
Toms River, NJ 08756
1-800-824-2232
www.iacea.org

> System of education for children and adults with physical and multiple disabilities; teaches a positive approach to learning which develops problem-solving and an active, independent, motivated approach to activities.

Lilli Nielsen Materials
Books and materials created by Lilli Nielsen, internationally known teacher of blind children, especially children with significant delays or additional disabilities; feature active learning approach to stimulate development in all areas. Available from:

LilliWorks	**Vision Associates**
1815 Encinal Ave.	2109 US Hwy 90 West Ste. 170 #312
Almeda, CA 94501	Lake City, FL 32055
510-814-9111	407-352-1200
www.lilliworks.com	www.visionkits.com

MOVE International (Mobility Opportunities Via Education)
1300 17th St. City Centre
Bakersfield, CA 93301-4533
1-800-397-6683
www.move-international.org

> Movement therapy program for people with severe disabilities to enable them to sit, stand, and walk more independently; programs throughout US and international.

Nordoff-Robbins Center for Music Therapy
82 Washington Square East, 4th fl.
NY, NY 10003
212-998-5151
www.education.nyu.edu/music/nrobbins

> Music therapy designed to help people with severe disabilities communicate and move more freely; programs throughout US and Europe.

North American Riding for the Handicapped Association (NARHA)
PO Box 33150
Denver, CO 80233
1-800-369-7433
www.narha.org

Information about therapeutic riding to enhance movement, posture, and communication for people with physical, emotional, and learning disabilities.

Perkins School for the Blind
175 North Beacon St.
Watertown, MA 02472
617-924-3434
www.perkins.org

Publishes *Perkins Activity and Resource Guide: A Handbook for Teachers and Parents of Students with Visual and Multiple Disabilities*

Toys for Special Children and Enabling Devices
385 Warburton Ave.
Hastings-on-Hudson, NY 10706
1-800-832-8697
www.enablingdevices.com

Toys and devices for children with physical impairments.

United Cerebral Palsy
1660 L St., NW, Suite 700
Washington DC 20036
1-800-872-5827
www.ucpa.org

Dedicated to enhancing the independence, productivity, inclusion, and self-determination of people with cerebral palsy and other disabilities; affiliates in most states.

DEAF-BLINDNESS

Deaf-Blind Perspectives
Teaching Research
345 N. Monmouth Ave.
Monmouth, OR 97361
503-838-8885
www.tr.wou.edu/tr/dbp

Journal focusing on issues important to deaf-blind people from birth to senior citizen and their service providers. Spans age range from birth to senior citizen. Includes articles on people who are cognitively able and those with cognitive disability.

DB-Link

The National Information Clearinghouse on Children Who Are Deaf-Blind

345 No. Monmouth Ave.

Monmouth, OR 97361

1-800-438-9376

www.tr.wou.edu/dblink

National information clearinghouse; information and referrals; national and state resource sheets.

Gallaudet University

800 Florida Ave. NE

Washington DC 20002

202-651-5000

www.gallaudet.edu

College for deaf/hard of hearing students. Catalog of books on sign language, the IEP, education of deaf-blind children; stories in sign language.

John Tracy Clinic

806 W. Adams Blvd.

Los Angeles, CA 90007-2505

1-800-522-4582

www.johntracyclinic.org

Correspondence courses for preschool deaf-blind children and their parents.

National Family Association for the Deaf-Blind (NFADB) and
Helen Keller National Center

111 Middle Neck Rd.

Sands Point, NY 11050

1-800-255-0411

www.nfadb.org

Networking, information, advocacy; college preparation program; job preparation and placement; National Technology Assistance program.

Perkins School for the Blind

175 No. Beacon St.

Watertown, MA 02472

617-924-3434

www.perkins.org

Information and curriculum materials.

State Deafblind Projects
www.tr.wou.edu/ntac/links.htm

Educational resources and support services for deaf-blind children.

INFORMATION ABOUT BLINDNESS/VISUAL IMPAIRMENT

American Foundation for the Blind (AFB)
11 Penn Plaza, Suite 300
New York, NY 10001
1-800-232-5463 (Information line)
1-800-232-3044 (Publications and Sales line)
www.afb.org

Books, pamphlets, and information on blindness in areas of education, literacy, technology, employment, and aging. Publishes *Journal of Visual Impairment and Blindness*.

American Self-Help Clearinghouse
http://mentalhelp.net/selfhelp/

Online Self-Help Sourcebook and directory of toll-free information and referral numbers.

Blind Children's Fund
311 W Broadway Suite 1
Mt. Pleasant, MI 48858
989-779-9966
www.blindchildrensfund.org

Information, resources, and materials to help parents and teachers teach and nurture their blind, visually impaired, and multiply disabled children. Publishes the *VIP Newsletter*.

Blind Children's Resource Center
www.blindchildren.org

Informative website featuring information about blindness/visual impairment, education and development, independent movement and travel, physical education, and more.

National Federation of the Blind (NFB)
1800 Johnson St.
Baltimore, MD 21230
410-659-9314
www.nfb.org

Organization of blind and visually impaired people, families, and friends working toward opportunity and equality for the blind. Information, videos, materials, networking opportunities, training. Scholarship program. Publishes *Braille Monitor* magazine. Houses the International Braille and Technology Center for the Blind. Parents Division (NOPBC); state chapters.

National Organization of Parents of Blind Children (NOPBC)
1800 Johnson St.
Baltimore, MD 21230
410-659-9314
www.nfb.org/nopbc.htm

National organization of parents, teachers, and friends of blind/VI children working to create a climate of opportunity at home, in school, and in the community. Helps parents gain understanding of blindness through contact with blind/VI adults. Publishes magazine *Future Reflections* for parents and teachers. Provides seminars, information, support, resources, training. Division of NFB; state chapters.

National Organization for Rare Disorders (NORD)
55 Kenosia Ave.
PO Box 1968
Danbury, CT 06813-1968
www.rarediseases.org

Information, rare disease data bank, organizations data bank.

HELPFUL BOOKS

CHILDREN WITH ADDITIONAL DISABILITIES

Early Learning Step by Step
Are You Blind?
Space and Self
The Comprehending Hand
Fiela Curriculum and other books by Lilli Nielsen available from:

Vision Associates
2109 US Hwy 90 West Ste. 170 #312
Lake City, FL 32055
407-352-1200
www.visionkits.com

Perkins Activity and Resource Guide: A Handbook for Teachers and Parents of Students with Visual and Multiple Disabilities by Kathy Heydt et al.
available from:

Perkins School for the Blind
175 North Beacon St.
Watertown, MA 02472
617-924-3434
www.perkins.org

EDUCATION AND BRAILLE

The Slate Book by Jennifer Dunnam
Handbook for Itinerant and Resource Teachers of Blind and Visually Impaired Students by Doris Willoughby and Sharon Duffy
both available from:

National Center for the Blind
Materials Center
1800 Johnson St.
Baltimore, MD 21230
410-659-9314
www.nfb.org

The Bridge to Braille: Reading and School Success for the Young Blind Child by Carol Castellano and Dawn Kosman
Because Books Matter: Reading Braille Books with Young Blind Children by Carol Castellano
Just Enough to Know Better: A Braille Primer by Eileen Curran
all available from:

National Braille Press
88 St. Stephen St.
Boston, MA 02115-4302
1-800-548-7323
www.nbp.org

Beginning with Braille: Firsthand Experiences with a Balanced Approach to Literacy by Anna Swenson
Burns Braille Transcription Dictionary by Mary Burns
Guidelines and Games for Teaching Efficient Braille Reading by Myrna Olson and Sally Mangold
all available from:

American Foundation for the Blind (AFB)
11 Penn Plaza, Suite 300
New York, NY 10001
1-800-232-3044
www.afb.org

Braille into the Next Millennium edited by Judith Dixon
available from:

National Library Service for the Blind and Physically Handicapped
1291 Taylor St., NW
Washington DC 20011
1-800-424-8567
www.loc.gov/nls

O&M/INDEPENDENT TRAVEL

Move It, by Richard Drouillard and Sherry Raynor
available from:

Blind Children's Fund
311 W Broadway Suite 1
Mt. Pleasant, MI 48858
989-779-9966
www.blindchildrensfund.org

Promoting Independent Movement and Travel in Blind Children: A Developmental Orientation & Mobility Approach by Joe Cutter
available from:

Information Age Publishing
PO Box 4967
Greenwich, CT 06830
203-661-7602
www.infoagepub.com

Modular Instruction for Independent Travel for Students Who Are Blind or Visually Impaired: Preschool through High School by Doris Willoughby and Sharon Monthei
Techniques Used by Blind Cane Travel Instructors—A Practical Approach by Maria Morais et al
both available from:

National Center for the Blind
Materials Center
1800 Johnson St.
Baltimore, MD 21230
410-659-9314
www.nfb.org

THE EXPERIENCE OF BLINDNESS/VISUAL IMPAIRMENT AND DISABILITY

Extraordinary People with Disabilities by Deborah Kent and Kathryn Quinlan
Out of print, but available in libraries and online.
Athletes with Disabilities by Deborah Kent
available from:

Scholastic Library Publishing/Children's Press
PO Box 1795
Danbury, CT 06810
1-800-621-1115
www.scholasticlibrary.com

Reflections from a Different Journey: What Adults with Disabilities Wish All Parents Knew edited by Stanley Klein and John Kemp
available from:

McGraw-Hill
2 Penn Plaza
New York, NY 10121
212-904-2000
www.books.mcgraw-hill.com

Julie and Brandon: Our Blind Friends
Activity and coloring book for sighted children.
The *Kernel Book* Series
Stories about blindness written by blind people.
All available from:

National Center for the Blind
Materials Center
1800 Johnson St.
Baltimore, MD 21230
410-659-9314
www.nfb.org

INDEPENDENT LIVING

Lifeskills: A Can-Do Program for Living with Blindness by Janiece Duffy
available from:

Janiece Duffy
1886 29th Ave. NW
New Brighton, MN 55112
651-639-1435

HELPFUL VIDEOS

Discovering the Magic of Reading: Elizabeth's Story
Opening Doors Through an Act to Promote the Education of the Blind
available from:

American Printing House for the Blind (APH)
1839 Frankfort Ave.
PO Box 6085
Louisville, KY 40206-0085
1-800-223-1839
www.aph.org

Power at Your Fingertips: An Introduction to Learning Braille
available from:

Visually Impaired Preschool Services (VIPS)
1906 Goldsmith La.
Louisville, KY 40218
1-888-636-8477
www.vips.org

Braille Is Beautiful Video Set
Braille Is Beautiful Curriculum Kit
That the Blind May Read
Jake and the Secret Code
It's Not So Different
all available from:

National Center for the Blind
Materials Center
1800 Johnson St.
Baltimore, MD 21230
410-659-9314
www.nfb.org

Teaching the Braille Slate and Stylus: A Manual for Mastery
available from:

Exceptional Teaching Aids
20102 Woodbine Ave.
Castro Valley, CA 94546
1-800-549-6999
www.exceptionalteaching.com

Understanding Braille Literacy
available from:

American Foundation for the Blind (AFB)
11 Penn Plaza, Suite 300
New York, NY 10001
1-800-232-3044
www.afb.org

Farther Than the Eye Can See, the story of blind mountaineer Erik Weihenmayer's successful climb of Mt. Everest
available from:

Serac Adventure Films
www.seracfilms.com

Locked Out, a story about a blind student and acceptance
available from:

AIMS Multimedia
20765 Superior St.
Chatsworth, CA 91311-4409
1-888-892-3484
www.aimsmultimedia.com

USING READERS

The following articles give firsthand accounts of the importance of having skill in using readers. All available online from www.nfb.org. Go to *Future Reflections* or *Braille Monitor*.

"The Care and Feeding of Readers," by Peggy Pinder, *Braille Monitor*, May 1993, Vol. 36, No. 5.

"Of Readers and Drivers and Responsibility," by Peggy Pinder Elliott and Barbara Cheadle, *Future Reflections*, Convention 1994, Vol. 13, No. 4.

"Using Readers on the Job," by Adrienne Asch, *Braille Monitor*, February 1992, Vol. 35, No. 2.

REFERENCES

American Printing House for the Blind (n.d.). *Distribution of eligible students based on the federal quota census of January 6, 2003 (Fiscal Year 2004).* Retrieved November 13, 2004, from http://sun1.aph.org/fedquotpgm/dist03.html

Castellano, C., & Kosman, D. (1997). *The bridge to braille: Reading and school success for the young blind child.* Baltimore: National Organization of Parents of Blind Children.

Cutter, J. (2004). Parents: Blind children's first mobility teachers [Special Issue— The Early Years]. *Future Reflections, 23*(2), 45.

Individuals with Disabilities Education Act (IDEA), 1997, § 614 (d) (3) (B) (iii).

Kent, D., & Quinlan, K. A. (1996). *Extraordinary people with disabilities.* Danbury, CT: Children's Press.

Koestler, F. A. (2004). *The unseen minority: A social history of blindness in the United States.* New York: AFB Press.

Nemeth, A. (1992). To light a candle with mathematics. In K. Jernigan (Ed.), *As the twig is bent* (pp. 109, 110). Baltimore: National Federation of the Blind.

Ryles, R. (2000). Braille as a predictor of success. In J. M. Dixon (Ed.), *Braille into the next millennium* (pp. 462-491). Washington, DC: National Library Service for the Blind and Physically Handicapped and Friends of Libraries for Blind and Physically Handicapped Individuals in North America.

Spungin, S. J. & D'Andrea, F. M. (2000). Braille literacy. In J. M. Dixon (Ed.), *Braille into the next millennium* (pp. 434-461). Washington, DC: National Library Service for the Blind and Physically Handicapped and Friends of Libraries for Blind and Physically Handicapped Individuals in North America.

Vermeij, G. (1997). *Privileged hands: A scientific life.* New York: W.H. Freeman.

Vermeij, G. (1994). To sea with a blind scientist. In K. Jernigan (Ed.), *Standing on one foot* (p. 81). Baltimore: National Federation of the Blind.

ABOUT THE AUTHOR

Carol Castellano is the co-author of *The Bridge to Braille: Reading and School Success for the Young Blind Child* and author of *Because Books Matter: Reading Braille Books with Young Blind Children* and many articles on the education and development of blind/VI children. Ms. Castellano makes presentations for parents and classroom teachers around the country. To arrange a workshop, guest lecture, or training, you may contact her at center@webspan.net.

INDEX

Page numbers in italics indicate illustrations.

CPSIA information can be obtained at www.ICGtesting.com
Printed in the USA
238036LV00001B/70/A

9 781593 114183